SUBMARINE DISASTERS

SUBMARINE DISASTERS

David Miller

The Lyons Press
Guilford, Connecticut
An imprint of The Globe Pequot Press

Copyright © 2006 Compendium Publishing Ltd.

First Lyons Press edition, 2006

The Lyons Press is an imprint of The Globe Pequot Press.

10 9 8 7 6 5 4 3 2 1

The Author

DAVID MILLER is a former officer in the British armed forces and
has seen service in the Falkland Islands, the Far East, and
Europe. He is a noted historian who has written more than fifty
books on naval affairs, military weapons, and warfare, ancient
and modern. He has also contributed to many specialty and
historical military magazines. For several years after leaving the
forces he was a staff writer on the *International Defense Review*
journal and an Editor with the Jane's Group of military directory
publishers. He is now a full-time defense author and
commentator.

Credits
Project Manager: Ray Bonds
Designer: Dave Ball
Diagrams: Mark Franklin
Photo Research: Anne and Rolf Lang
Printed and bound in China

Additional captions
Page 1: Saved! A British submariner on a training exercise
emerges from the depths of the ocean; his protective suit will
keep him afloat and warm until a surface rescue ship arrives.

Pages 2-3: Rescuers struggle to raise the hulk of USS *Squalus*
(SS-192), May 1939, but many of the crew had already been
saved, using the McCann Rescue Chamber.

ISBN-13: 978-1-59228-815-1
ISBN-10: 1-59228-815-4

Library of Congress Cataloging-in-Publication Data
is available on file.

Above: So near, yet so far – rescuers failed to save most of the crew of the British Royal Navy's HMS *Thetis*, even though the stern was clear of the surface. *Thetis* sank on June 1, 1939, only days after *Squalus* (see previous page) but the losses led to a fundamental reappraisal of the failure, and, in turn, to major improvements in both rescue equipment and procedures.

CONTENTS

Main image: The U.S. Navy Los Angeles attack submarine USS *La Jolla* (SSN-701) with the Deep Submergence Rescue Vehicle *Mystic* (DSRV-1) attached. *Mystic* was specifically designed to fill the need for an improved means of rescuing the crew of a submarine immobilized on the ocean floor. It can operate independently of surface conditions or under ice for rapid response to an accident anywhere in the world.

Above: So near, yet so far – rescuers failed to save most of the crew of the British Royal Navy's HMS *Thetis*, even though the stern was clear of the surface. *Thetis* sank on June 1, 1939, only days after *Squalus* (see previous page) but the losses led to a fundamental reappraisal of the failure, and, in turn, to major improvements in both rescue

CONTENTS

Main image: The U.S. Navy Los Angeles attack submarine USS *La Jolla* (SSN-701) with the Deep Submergence Rescue Vehicle *Mystic* (DSRV-1) attached. *Mystic* was specifically designed to fill the need for an improved means of rescuing the crew of a submarine immobilized on the ocean floor. It can operate independently of surface conditions or under ice for rapid response to an accident anywhere in the world.

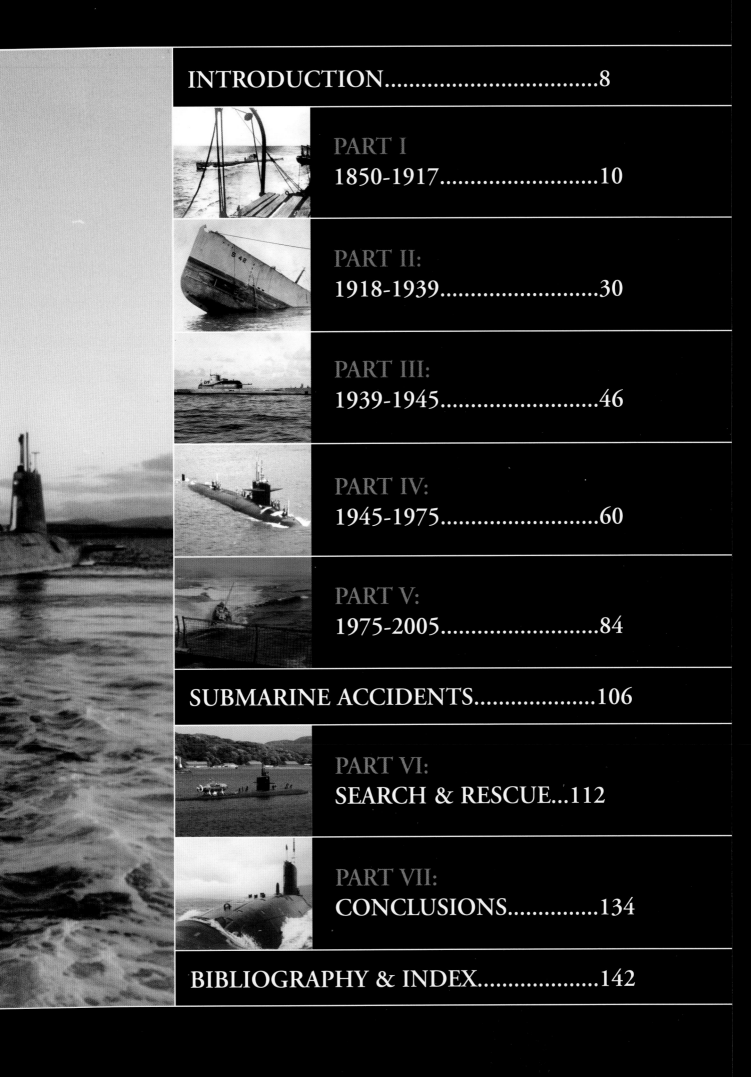

Introduction

Since the start of serious submarine operations in the 19th Century, there has been something about their losses that set them apart in the public consciousness. The specter of men fighting for their lives in a metal tomb deep under the ocean's surface grips the public imagination, as was shown as recently as May 2003 in the tragic loss of the Russian submarine, *Kursk*.

Other major tragedies—for example, natural disasters like the *tsunami* in December 2004, or earthquakes, a surface ship sinking in a storm, or the crash of an aircraft or train—all happen very suddenly and the event is usually over by the time the media reaches the scene. With a submarine, however, trapped men can endure for some time and, if they are not rescued, death is slow and drawn out. The only real parallel is with mining disasters, where rescuers on the surface struggle to reach men trapped far underground.

There are six main reasons for submarine losses. The first two are enemy action and scuttling, the latter almost invariably relating to avoiding capture by the enemy, but both are concerned with war and not the subject of this book.

The first category unrelated to enemy action is the hazard of the sea, such as running aground, hitting rocks or foundering in a storm, dangers that face every mariner in both peace and war. Second is collision, and submarines on or near the surface have been particularly susceptible to colliding with surface ships, almost always because the crew of the latter failed to see them, since the submarine lies low in the water, is painted in unobtrusive colors, and its navigation lights are difficult to see.

There have been many losses due to equipment malfunction. Thus, crews have been overcome by fumes when seawater reached the batteries, the boat has been blown apart in an explosion caused by the ignition of pockets of hydrogen, or, in the early days of snorkeling, boats were lost due to malfunctioning of the snorkel system. In more recent years, a number of Soviet submarines have been lost due to nuclear accidents. Human error, too, has been the cause of many losses—for example, by someone forgetting to close a vent, or a dockyard worker failing to seal a joint properly.

There is also the loss due to "unknown causes," where a submarine has sailed on patrol, perhaps made its presence at sea known by visual sightings or by radio report, and then vanished without any form of distress signal.

In addition there is a minor category, known as "constructive total loss," an awkward bureaucratic term meaning that the submarine has been damaged, in a collision for example, but has survived and returned to port. On being surveyed, however, the damage has been regarded as so extensive that it would not be worthwhile undertaking repairs, so the submarine is written-off and scrapped.

This is the story of the brave men of every navy who go down in submarines, and of some of them who failed to return to tell their tale. It is also dedicated to the men who have designed rescue systems and equipment, and to those courageous souls who have risked their lives in their efforts to save those of others trapped beneath the oceans.

Right: The loss of USS *S.48* (SS-159) and the saving of its crew were due to opposing characteristics of human nature. The loss was the result of a misunderstanding and neglect in the shipyard, where a manhole cover was not secured properly. Having analyzed the situation after sinking, the captain so manipulated the water in the buoyancy tanks that he brought the bow above the surface, following which the crew crawled to safety through a torpedo tube.

PART I: 1850-1917

Left: During World War One, the Imperial German Navy's U-boat fleet brought home the grim reality and the seriousness of the threat of submarine warfare. This is *U-29*, seen from one of her victims, but she met her own end early in the war, on March 18, 1915, when she was rammed and sunk by the British HMS *Dreadnought*, with the loss of every member of her crew, the only known occasion when a battleship has sunk a submarine.

PART I: 1850-1917

In the century leading up to J. P. Holland's development of a workable submarine in the 1890s there were dozens of individuals who designed and built their own underwater vessels and then tested them. But they were wrestling with a medium whose nature was poorly understood and using materials and construction methods that were not up to the task. They were also faced by three fundamental difficulties: how to make the submarine descend into the depths and then, most importantly, come back up again; and how to propel it while it was down there. The question of recovering the intrepid submariners if something went wrong featured well down the list of priorities. Fortunately, most submarines accommodated only one or two people, so when the contraption failed to surface the death bill was fairly small.

The English boat *Maria* disappeared under the waves off Plymouth, England, on June 20, 1774, and those meeting similar fates were the American *Phillip* (1851), French *Petit* (1834), and Spanish *Cervo* (1831). In America the *Hunley* established a new practice whereby sunken submarines could be recovered, bodies removed, damage repaired, and the boat returned to service. *Hunley* still

holds the record for having done this no fewer than three times, killing thirty-five men in the process.

The general idea was that if anything went wrong the entire submarine would be recovered, with the crew being released once it was on the surface, although one of the earliest pioneers demonstrated that individual escape was perfectly possible. Indeed, the sinking of the German boat *Brandtaucher* in 1851 is a prime example of how a potential disaster can be turned into a triumph by one man remaining cool, making sensible plans, and keeping his crew under firm control.

Wilhelm Bauer (1822-75) was particularly interested in submarines and after several attempts he built the *Brandtaucher* (= diving incendiary), which was 26 feet 6 inches long, displaced 30.5 tons, and carried a crew of three. Two men turned a handwheel driving the propeller, while the third was the captain, who controlled depth, trim and direction from a conning position in the bows.

On February 1, 1851, Bauer and two men undertook the first trial and had reached a depth of 30 feet when the water pressure began to distort the frame, the handwheel came off its bearings, and the boat sank, bottoming at a depth of fifty-three feet. The two hands began to panic,

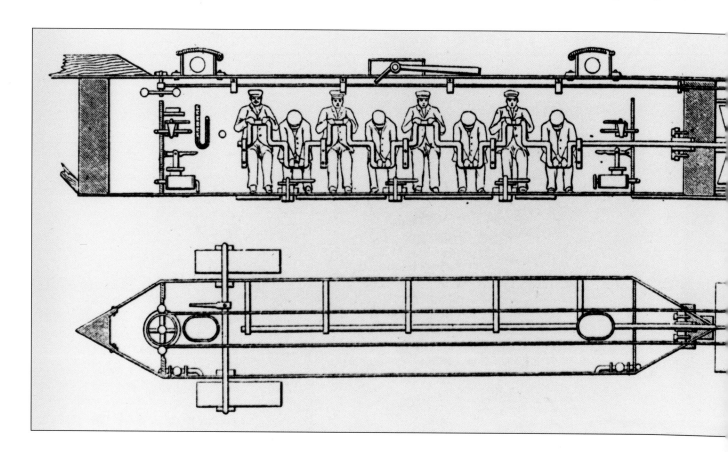

Right: The German submarine *Brandtaucher*, designed and built by the great pioneer Wilhelm Bauer. The boat sank February 1, 1851, settling at a depth of some 53 feet, but Bauer kept his head and controlled his two man crew, forcing them to await the equalization of pressure before leaving the boat in the first ever successful escape from a sunken submarine.

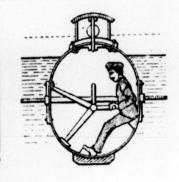

Left: Known after its inventor as the *Hunley*, this submarine was built for the Confederate States Navy during the American Civil War. The boat was powered by seven men (not eight as in this early drawing) turning a crank. She sank three times, killing her entire crew on each occasion. She was recovered and returned to service after the first two disasters.

but Bauer kept calm, explained his plan and then kept them waiting for no less than six-and-a-half hours while the water height gradually increased until the internal and external pressures were equal. Bauer then opened the hatch and the three men shot to the surface, astonishing the spectators, who had long since given up hope.

Most submarines built up to about 1910 were powered by gasoline engines, introducing a new hazard, since fumes tended to build up in the closed space of the hull, particularly if the crew were careless when refueling, and a spark from the electrical machinery then ignited it. The British had two such

Above: French submarine *Gymnote*, with most of the hull hidden below the surface. Completed in 1888, she became one of the first of many submarines to sink in dock (Toulon, June 19, 1907). Such cases were almost invariably the result of human error.

gasoline explosions: the *A.5*, with 7 killed, 12 hurt (February 16, 1905), and the *C.8*, 3 killed, 13 hurt (June 13, 1907). One outcome of these experiences was that British submarines started to carry white mice that were reputed to squeak loudly when they detected gasoline fumes.

In addition, the *A.9* had some men suffocated by gasoline vapor (July 13, 1908) although this time there was no spark to ignite what was clearly a very dense concentration. Another gasoline explosion took place but without causing deaths—on the Japanese *No 1*, March 4, 1903, in which four submariners were injured. The Italian *Foca*

Right: The British A-class was based on the U.S. Navy's Holland design, but with improvements based on operational experience. This is *A.11*, which survived, but four of her sisters were lost, three being rammed by surface vessels and one foundering.

Above: Most early submarines were powered by gasoline engines and like many of them, the Japanese *No 1*, seen here, suffered an explosion (March 4, 1904) in which four of the crew were injured, but none fatally.

Below: The E-class was the backbone of the Royal Navy's submarine force from 1912 onwards and throughout World War One. Although diesel-powered, *E.5* of this class suffered a major engine-room explosion in 1913, in which three sailors died.

Above: British *A.1* was rammed and sunk by a merchant ship, SS *Berwick Castle*, March 18, 1904, with the loss of all eleven crew. She was raised but never recommissioned and was later sunk as a target.

Above: The French *Farfadet* was powered only by accumulators that had to be recharged in harbor. She was sunk accidentally at Bizerta in 1905 with the loss of fourteen lives, but was raised, docked (as seen here), and later recommissioned.

(April 26, 1909) and Russian *Drakon* (August 14, 1909) were also destroyed by gasoline explosions (14 and 17 killed, respectively). Another British submarine, *E.5,* which had diesel engines, suffered an engine-room explosion in which three were killed (June 8, 1913).

As the number of submarines increased, another hazard came to light. Submarines on the surface were very low, dark and difficult to see, especially at night or in poor visibility, and their navigation lights were of little help. As a result, several boats were run down by merchant ships, the British losing no fewer than three: *A.1,* 11 dead (March 18, 1904); *C.11,* 13 dead (July 14, 1909); and *B.2,* 15 dead (October 4, 1912). Other navies suffered similarly: Russia, *Delfin,* 21 dead (June 29, 1904), and France, *Pluviose,* 27 dead (May 26, 1910).

Lookouts on merchant ships might have had some excuse for not being aware of the danger their ships presented to small submarines, but warship crews ought to have done better. Three submarines were lost to naval ships, two of them to battleships, the Russian *Kambala* (June 12, 1909—23 dead), and the French *Vendemaire* (June 8, 1912—24 dead), while the British *A.3* was hit by a destroyer with the appropriate name of HMS *Hazard* (February 2, 1912—14 dead). A collision with a fellow submarine could be equally destructive, as discovered by the French *Calypso* and *Circe* which collided with each other on July 7, 1914, resulting in three deaths, although twenty-three men survived.

Above: Australian submarine HMAS *AE-1* was taking part in the New Guinea campaign in September 1914 when she disappeared with all hands. Where and why she was lost remain enduring mysteries, and repeated attempts to find the wreck have all failed.

WORLD WAR ONE (1914-1918)

The Great War saw the first large-scale use of submarines in combat, and they were employed with great vigor by most major navies, with German U-boats in particular leaving an indelible mark on naval history. Large numbers of submarines were lost to enemy action, but, in addition, losses due to the hazards of the sea continued.

OPERATIONAL LOSS

The war introduced a new category that would become all too familiar: "Operational loss; cause unknown." These incidents involved boats that sailed on a combat mission and then simply disappeared, taking their complete crews—and the story of what had happened to them—to their graves. In peacetime, navies could seek the wrecks, but in wartime this was rarely possible. A few such losses were explained when the war was over but, despite examination of enemy anti-submarine reports, seven World War One losses remain unexplained to this day.

In August 1914 Australia mounted an operation to capture German New Guinea, dispatching a force which included the submarines *AE-1* and *AE-2*. On September 14, *AE-1* and the destroyer HMAS *Parramatta* divided a search area between them. Although there was a mist, *Parramatta*'s lookouts saw *AE-1* at 1430 and again at about 1530, when she appeared to be heading back to their temporary base at Herbertshöhe. When *Parramatta* returned to port at 1930, however, it was realized that *AE-1* had not arrived and the alarm was raised. Extensive searches failed to discover any trace of the missing submarine—not even an oil slick. There have been several searches since, but no convincing explanation of her disappearance has ever been given.

Left: The German *U-52* suffered a mysterious explosion in port, October 29, 1917, in which five men were killed. The blast occurred in the after torpedo room but the cause was never established.

Four similar losses took place in the Mediterranean: two German submarines—*UB-3* in May 1915 and *UB-44* in August 1916—one Austro-Hungarian, *U-30*, in August 1917, and one Italian, *W-4*, the same month. Another loss was the German *UB-65*, which disappeared with all hands off south-west Ireland on July 10, 1918.

The German submarine *Bremen* was not strictly a naval vessel, having been built as a commercial transport and operated by a civil company for trade with the United States. She sailed on her maiden trading voyage in late 1916 but disappeared without trace in the north Atlantic, cause unknown.

EXPLOSIONS

As in the prewar period, explosions continued. USS *E-2* (SS-25) was in the Brooklyn Navy Yard on January 15, 1916, where hydrogen gas was being vented from her storage battery. Ventilation was poor and the gas was allowed to accumulate; it was then ignited by a spark, resulting in a violent explosion in which five men were killed and seven injured.

The German *U-52* also suffered a major explosion in port on October 29, 1917, when there was a huge explosion in her torpedo room, although why a torpedo should have exploded in dock is unclear. Again, five men were killed.

Two submarines exploded while at sea. The disaster that befell the Japanese *No 4* was the result of a gasoline explosion, with two men killed. The boat sank, but was later recovered, repaired, and returned to service. The French submarine *Diane* was on the surface, escorting a sailing ship at night in the Bay of Biscay on February 11, 1918. Suddenly, those aboard the sailing ship observed a major explosion in which *Diane* disappeared—there were no survivors. *Diane* was not under attack and the reason for the explosion was never established. She could have been charging her battery and the explosion may have been due to the ignition of an accumulation of hydrogen gas.

Above: French submarine *Diane* at her launch, September 30, 1916. On February 11, 1918, she blew apart while on the surface, with the loss of her entire crew; no explanation has ever been found.

Above: USS *F-1* (SS-20) lying aground at Watsonville, California, in 1912. She ran aground on October 11 and after causing considerable local interest, as seen here, was refloated on October 18 and returned to service, but was later lost for good (see inset).

COLLISIONS BETWEEN SUBMARINES

There were five collisions between submarines during 1917/1918, three of them involving British boats, one of which, the British *E.36*, was hit by *E.43* off Harwich on January 19, 1917, and sank with the loss of all hands.

In December that year, three U.S. Navy F-class boats, *F-1* (SS-20), *F-2* (SS-21), and *F-3* (SS-22), were based at San Pedro, California. On December 17 they took part in a combined training mission. As was normal at the time, they were not fitted with radio and could only communicate on the surface by flag or light. They were sailing on the surface in line abreast off La Jolla, when, at about 1850, the leader sent a visual message to change course to avoid a fog bank ahead. The message reached the second boat, but was not seen by *F-1*, which continued on the previous course and disappeared into the fog. Some ten minutes later *F-3* appeared out of the fog and hit *F-1* on her port side,

almost at right angles, its sharp bow ramming straight through *F-1*'s ballast tanks and pressure hull. The five men on the bridge, including the commanding officer, were thrown into the water, but the nineteen men inside the hull never had a chance, the boat taking less than ten seconds to disappear below the surface. The wreck was located and photographed in the 1970s, but is designated a registered grave and remains untouched.

Left: USS *F-1* (SS-20) was rammed and sunk with the loss of 19 lives, December 17, 1917. Found by chance in 1972 by the oceanographic vessel, USNS *De Steiguer* (T-AGOR-12), the submerged wreck, seen here with an open hatch, is now a registered memorial.

The other collisions between British boats occurred early in January 1918, and involved K-class submarines in a sequence of incidents referred to as the "Battle" of May Island (see box).

COLLISIONS BETWEEN SUBMARINES AND SURFACE SHIPS

Dykkeren was a small Danish submarine, carrying a crew of one officer and eight men, and powered only by batteries, which had to be recharged in port. She was used only for training. On October 9, 1916, she conducted a routine dive near Copenhagen, accompanied by a small steamer, *Sleipner*. Shortly after *Dykkeren* dived at 1330 *Sleipner's* lookouts saw a Norwegian steamer, SS *Vesla*, approaching and warned her of the submerged submarine. Norwegian reaction was slow and she struck the submarine, tearing a 12-foot hole in her engine room. *Sleipner* raised the alarm, buoyed the spot, and informed the guardship, *Guldborgsund*, which signaled naval headquarters. By chance, *Dykkeren's* previous commanding officer, Commander Brockdorff, was aboard *Guldborgsund*, and was not only a fully qualified diver but also had his diving equipment with him.

Nobody was injured inside *Dykkeren*, and Lieutenant Christiansen ordered watertight doors closed, main tanks blown, and drop keel released. But this was in vain and the submarine bottomed at a depth of about thirty feet. Twelve lifejackets were carried, but four were in the flooded area and two were faulty, leaving six for nine men. The three without breathing gear escaped first, entering the conning tower with Christiansen, who was wearing breathing gear. Christiansen closed the lower hatch, flooded up, and opened the upper hatch, and the three men ascended to the surface, to be picked up by *Sleipner*. So far, so good, but when Christiansen ordered the crew in the control room to drain the conning tower for the next escape the drop in pressure was so rapid that he expired within seconds. When the men below opened the hatch they were horrified to discover his dead body.

The remaining five submariners had no idea what had gone wrong but refused to use the conning tower again. They also detected chlorine as the seawater reached the battery, and they moved into the forward torpedo room, securing the watertight door behind them. At about this time Brockdorff made his first dive, but was foiled by the submarine's angle and the strong currents. The civilian salvage vessel *Kattegat* was in position within three hours and a diver attached an airline, which started to pump clean air into the boat. Brockdorff then descended again and made contact with the survivors, exchanging Morse code messages using hammers.

Cables were then attached to the sunken submarine and *Kattegat* raised her slowly to the surface. The conning tower surfaced at 2330, but there was another snag when *Kattegat's* crane was unable to raise *Dykkeren* high enough, and the forward hatch remained a tantalizing twelve inches below the surface. Undeterred, the rescuers surrounded the hatch with sacks full of sawdust, creating a watertight dam (nobody has ever explained where the sawdust came from!), and once this was high enough the hatch was opened and the five survivors made their way to safety. It was a very efficient rescue operation, marred only by the death of Lieutenant Christiansen.

The French submarine *Prairial* was launched in 1907.

On the night of April 28/29, 1918, the boat was on patrol off the port of Le Havre, accompanied by a patrol vessel, *Chasseur II*. In the early hours there was a fog and poor visibility, and at 0348 she was hit by the British steamer, SS *Tropic*. *Prairial* sank after only two minutes, taking nineteen men to their deaths; seven survived.

UC-91, a training boat in the Baltic, was hit by the German-registered passenger ship *Alexandra Woermann* (3,757 tons) on September 5, 1918. The reasons for the accident are not known, but seventeen men were killed,

while a further fourteen survived. The hulk was raised on September 6 by the salvage vessel *Vulkan*, and was repaired and returned to service.

On February 1, 1918, the British submarine *K.17* was sunk with the loss of forty-eight lives during the "Battle"

Below: Imperial German Navy *UC-91*, a Type UC-III minelayer, was employed on training when hit by a German passenger ship in the Baltic, September 5, 1918; 17 died, 19 survived. No picture of that boat survives, but *UC-103* (nearest camera) was identical in all respects.

Above: The British steam-powered K-class suffered many accidents. *K.13* was one that sank but was recovered and had her "unlucky" number changed to *K.22*; then, unlike many others in this unfortunate class, she survived to be scrapped in 1926.

Below: USS *F-4* (SS-23), lost off Hawaii March 25, 1914, lies between the camels used to refloat her. All 21 crew died; once their bodies had been given a proper burial it was found that corrosion had caused a major leak.

of May Island (see box). On October 21 that year, the submarine *UB-89* was hit by the German cruiser *Frankfort* in the Jade River and sank with the loss of seven lives, while twenty-four were saved.

DIVING LOSSES

USS *F.4* (SS-23) was on a diving exercise off Pearl Harbor on March 25, 1915, when her crew became unable to control her and she sank to the bottom at a depth of some 300 feet. All twenty-one aboard perished, but the boat was recovered some three weeks later and an investigation established that corrosion in a battery tank had resulted in a major leak.

The British K-class submarines were steam-powered, requiring two stacks to be raised, while the high temperatures in the boiler room needed four ventilators open. On January 29, 1917, *K.13* conducted a practice dive in the Gareloch,

Scotland, carrying her normal crew of fifty-three, plus the captain (Goodhart) and engineer officer of *K.14*, plus twenty-five civilian officials, a total of eighty men.

K.13's captain, Commander Herbert, ordered a dive at about 1545, but within seconds was told that the engine room was flooding. He ordered immediate counter-measures, but it was too late and the boat sank until it rested on the bottom at a depth of fifty-five feet. Herbert checked his crew to discover that just forty-nine men were alive; the remaining thirty-one, all aft, must have already been dead.

Right: British Commander Goodhart (seen here as lieutenant-commander) was a passenger aboard HMS *K.13* when she flooded and sank. Goodhart volunteered to escape and inform the rescuers of the situation, but was trapped in the wheelhouse and drowned.

On the surface, the alarm was raised at about 1600, but responses were slow and confused, the first rescue boat not sailing until about 2200, followed shortly afterwards by two salvage tugs. When they arrived, one tug was found to have a diving suit but no diver, while the other had neither. A civilian diver eventually arrived and descended to the submarine, where he exchanged Morse messages with the survivors, who told him that "all was well" (something of an overstatement).

Inside the submarine, Herbert and Goodhart decided the latter should escape with details of the situation and a list of survivors. Both entered the tower, where Herbert controlled the flooding, but when they opened the upper hatch the air pressure was so great that not only was Goodhart swept out, but so, too, was Herbert, although this proved beneficial to him, since Goodhart's body was later found lodged inside the wheelhouse.

Herbert told those on the surface what was going on and persuaded them to give priority to an air hose. This was attached at about 1800, but was blocked and had to be disconnected, unblocked and replaced. Clean air finally reached the survivors at about 0100 on January 31, some thirty-six hours after the boat had sunk. Compressed air bottles were recharged and tanks blown at about 0300. This raised the bows to about eight feet below the surface. A wide-bore hose was then secured to a ventilator, voice conversations replaced Morse code, and various supplies were passed down, including food and drink.

Next, the bows were raised to enable the men to crawl out through the torpedo tubes, but the stern slipped on the seabed and the tube mouths remained some two to three inches below the surface. The situation was now desperate, so a hole was cut through the bows, starting at 2000 and taking just over an hour. It was a complete success, and shortly after 2100 the forty-seven men began to leave the boat, having endured a remarkable fifty-seven hours of incarceration.

When *K.13* was recovered it was established that not only were the boiler-room ventilators open but that the engine room indicators showed this to be so. How this came about was never ascertained, since the engineer officer died, but the subsequent inquiry placed the entire blame on his shoulders.

CSS HUNLEY

DISPLACEMENT: submerged n/k.

DIMENSIONS: length 40 feet, beam 4 feet.

PROPULSION: 7-man manual.

PERFORMANCE (ESTIMATED): surface 3 knots; submerged 2 knots; depth 30 feet.

ARMAMENT: 1 x spar torpedo.

CREW: 8.

Designed and built in the Confederacy during the American Civil War, the *Hunley* consisted of a wooden frame coated with steel plates, with two watertight hatches and a primitive, fixed snorkel tube extending some four feet above the hull. Propulsion was by a propeller driven, through a reduction gear, by seven men turning a hand crank. The commander stood at the front, controlling the vessel by means of a rudder and forward-mounted hydroplanes. The weapon was a large explosive charge mounted at the tip of a 17-foot long iron tube.

The *Hunley* sank three times during training, all due to water washing over the open forward hatch, and resulting in the deaths of twenty-three men. She was raised, cleaned and recommissioned after each sinking, while increasing amounts of money attracted yet further crews. On February 17, 1864, *Hunley* attacked and sank the warship USS *Housatonic*, but somehow she was herself sunk, whether by accident or not has never been established.

Right: The low height of CSS *Hunley*'s access trunks allowed little freeboard, and explains how she came to be swamped so easily.

IJNS No 6

DISPLACEMENT: submerged 63 tons.

DIMENSIONS: length (oa) 26 feet 6 inches, beam 6 feet 7 inches.

PROPULSION: one gasoline engine; one electric motor; one shaft.

PERFORMANCE: surface 9 knots; submerged 4 knots; depth 100 feet.

ARMAMENT: one 45cm (bow); 1 torpedo.

CREW: 16.

On April 15, 1910, the Japanese submarine *No 6* disappeared during a test in Hiroshima Bay. When it was recovered the following day the crew were dead but the commanding officer, Lieutenant Sakuma, had left a record of exactly what happened in one of the most moving documents in submarine history (reproduced here in part, translated).

"...while making a gasoline dive the boat sank lower than was intended, and in our attempt to close the valve the chain broke. We endeavored to stop the inrush of water with our hands, but too late, the water entered at the rear and the boat sank...The water submerged the electric generator, put out the light, and the electric wires were burned. In a few minutes bad gas was generated, making it difficult for us to breathe...

"The electric current has become useless, gas cannot be generated, and the hand pump is our only hope. The vessel is in darkness, and I note this down by the light through the conning tower at 11:45 A. M.

"The crew are now wet and it is extremely cold. It is my opinion that men embarking in submarines must possess the qualities of coolness and nerve, and must be extremely painstaking; they must be brave and daring in their handling of the boat. People may laugh at the opinion in view of my failure, but the statement is true.

"We have worked hard to pump out the water, but the boat is still in the same position. It is now twelve o'clock. The depth of water here is about ten fathoms.

"The crew of a submarine should be selected from the bravest, the coolest, or they will be of little use in time of crisis—in such as we are now. My brave men are doing their best...

"A word to His Majesty the Emperor. It is my earnest hope that Your Majesty will supply the means of living to the poor families of the crew. This is my only desire, and I am so anxious to have it fulfilled...It is now 12:30 P.M. My breathing is so difficult and painful. I thought I could blow out gasoline, but I am intoxicated with it...it is now 12:40 p.m."

Lieutenant Sakuma had acted, in every respect, in the finest traditions of the sea.

Right: Lieutenant Sakuma, Imperial Japanese Navy, composed one of the most moving farewell notes ever written as he and his crew died aboard submarine *No 6*.

E.4/E.41

DISPLACEMENT: submerged 807 tons.

DIMENSIONS: length 181 feet, beam 23 feet.

PROPULSION: diesel-electric.

PERFORMANCE: surface 15 knots; submerged 10 knots; depth 100 feet.

ARMAMENT: 5 x 18-inch torpedo tubes (10 torpedoes); 1 x 12-pounder gun.

CREW: 31.

During a surface exercise off Harwich, on the east coast of England, on August 15, 1916, the British submarines *E.4* and *E.41* collided with each other, with *E.4* sinking immediately with the loss of all hands. Aboard *E.41* some twenty-four men managed to jump clear before she sank, but seven went down with their submarine, which came to rest at a depth of forty-five feet.

Six of these seven men waited quietly in the control room until the incoming water had equalized the pressure sufficiently for them to open the conning tower hatch, whereupon they all escaped, reached the surface and were quickly rescued. Petty Officer Brown had gone into the engine room to ensure there was nobody left there and when he returned to the control room it was empty, with the lower conning tower hatch closed. Quite alone and with only an electric emergency lamp to help him, Brown kept his head and spent some two hours in opening the engine room hatch, which opened inwards. He was eventually successful and escaped to the surface, where he was picked up by a waiting destroyer. It was a triumph of individual coolness in the face of great danger.

Above: Having collided with *E.4*, seven men went down with *E.41* (center), but all escaped, including one who remained for two hours on his own.

"BATTLE" OF MAY ISLAND

CLASS: K.

DISPLACEMENT: submerged 2,565 tons.

DIMENSIONS: length 338 feet, beam 27 feet.

PROPULSION: steam-electric.

PERFORMANCE: surface 24 knots, submerged 9 knots; diving depth 200 feet.

ARMAMENT: 10 x 21-inch torpedo tubes (18 torpedoes); 2 x 4-inch, 2 x 3-inch guns.

CREW: 59.

Late afternoon on January 31, 1918, forty British warships sailed from the Firth of Forth, Scotland, to participate in an exercise, led by the commanding admiral aboard HMS *Courageous*. Following were:

- 13th Submarine Flotilla (Captain Leir): HMS *Ithuriel* (destroyer): submarines *K.11*, *K.12*, *K.14*, *K.17*, *K.22*.
- 2nd Battle Squadron: four battle cruisers, 10 destroyers.
- 12th Submarine Flotilla (Captain Little): HMS *Fearless* (cruiser); submarines *K.3*, *K.4*, *K.6*, *K.7*.
- 5th Battle Squadron: three battleships, 10 destroyers.

Note that submarine flotilla commanders were aboard surface warships. The ships steamed at 19 knots, with five miles (in effect, fifteen minutes) between groups; all were blacked-out and radio silence was imposed. There was a light wind and an intermittent mist.

ACCIDENT 1

Abreast May Island, *Ithuriel*, leading 13th Flotilla, spotting two minesweepers approaching inbound, reduced speed and turned to port, followed by *K.11* and *K.17*. Next in line was *K.14*, whose crew realized it was closing too rapidly on *K.17* and turned to starboard, unseen by *K.12* which continued on the original course. But *K.14*'s helm jammed so that she turned in a circle and was recrossing the original track when *K.22* hit her broadside on. *K.14* and *K.22* implemented damage-control procedures while *Fearless*, *K.11*, *K.17* and *K.12* continued seawards.

ACCIDENT 2

K.22 rigged emergency lights, but fifteen minutes later 2nd Battle Squadron arrived to find *K.14* and *K.22* directly across their path. All but *Inflexible* avoided them, but she hit *K.22* with a glancing blow, causing further damage.

NEARLY ACCIDENT 3

Meanwhile, Captain Leir in *Ithuriel* learned of the collision and turned to assist, followed by *K.11*, *K.17*, and *K.12*. Leir turned on *Ithuriel's* navigation lights, but 2nd Battle Squadron failed to see them, although, despite very near misses, the two groups passed through each other unscathed.

ACCIDENT 4

12th Submarine Flotilla, following the battle cruisers, avoided *K.14* and *K.22*, but did not know that the remainder of 13th Flotilla was now heading inbound. The two flotillas met head-on just off May Island and *Fearless* rammed *K.17*, which sank in about eight minutes; this gave enough time for most of her crew to abandon ship. The submarines following *Fearless* turned to avoid this new collision but *K.6* rammed *K.4* square on; the latter was virtually cut in two and sank with all hands.

Above: British cruiser HMS *Fearless* after her collision with submarine *K.17* in the "Battle of May Island." Fortunately, *K.17*'s crew had time to abandon before their boat sank.

ACCIDENT 5

At this point 5th Battle Squadron and attendant destroyers, aware of the initial *K.14/K.22* collision but not of the subsequent accidents, steamed through the melee. Tragically, several destroyers passed through the area where the *K.17* survivors were swimming, killing many; only nine were rescued, one dying shortly afterwards.

SUMMARY

In this appalling sequence, 107 lives were lost (*K.4*—59; *K.17*—48), two submarines were sunk, and three submarines and a flotilla leader were damaged.

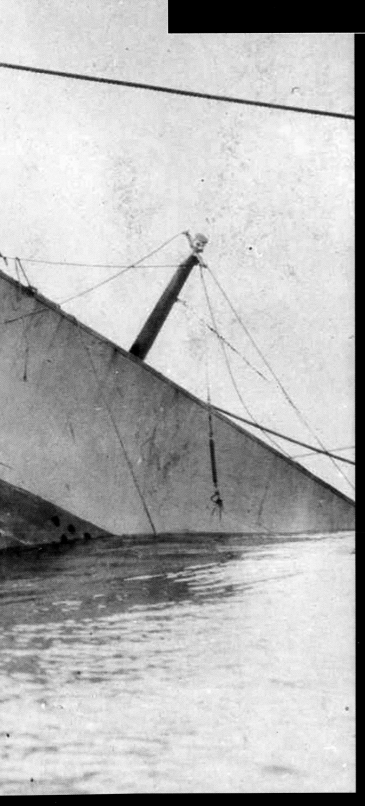

PART II: 1918-1939

Left: The bows of USS *S.48* (SS-159) rise above the waters of Long Island Sound. All 41 men aboard escaped through the port forward torpedo tube, which was precisely 21 inches in diameter, leaving no room for large or overweight crewmen.

PART II: 1918-1939

At the end of the Great War in 1918 the world's navies tried to agree to limits on future shipbuilding programs, with the British making a somewhat forlorn bid to have submarines banned altogether. This inevitably failed and the subsequent Washington Naval Treaty (1923) contained no provisions on submarines, while the London Naval Treaty (1930) managed only to limit individual new submarines to 2,032 metric tons. The treaties soon became worthless, however, not least because the Germans, who were not bound by either of these two treaties, began construction of a new U-boat fleet, and the major navies braced themselves for a new war.

HUMAN ERROR

During this inter-war period there were several submarine disasters, but in not one was an enemy involved, only the sea. Many totally avoidable mistakes played an unfortunately frequent role, being responsible, in one way or another, for the loss of 296 lives and

Above: USS *S.19* (SS-124) ran aground on the Massachusetts coast, January 13, 1925. Here an auxiliary waits for an opportunity to refloat her, which was eventually successful, although she never returned to service.

Right: USS *S.48* (SS-159) seen at sea after she had been sunk, recovered and refitted. She was one of four S-class boats known as the "2nd Lake Type" and was armed with five 21-inch torpedo tubes and one 4-inch/50 caliber deck gun.

eleven boats, although most of the latter were recovered and returned to service.

Two boats sank while undergoing trials prior to commissioning, when the line of responsibility between the naval crew and dockyard staff was blurred. In the case of the British *Thetis* this resulted in incorrect trim, leading to various complications (see box). The American submarine *S.48* (SS-159) undertook a pre-commissioning diving trial on December 7, 1921, but a ballast tank manhole cover had not been properly secured, so that, as soon as she dived, several aft compartments flooded and the boat sank in sixty feet of water. The captain blew the forward tanks, raising the bows above the water, and all forty-one aboard crawled through a torpedo tube and escaped, without any outside assistance, to be picked up by a waiting tug—a most remarkable exploit.

The remaining boats (of the eleven that sank due to human error) were in service when they were lost. USS *R.6* (SS-83) suffered a torpedo tube malfunction at San Pedro, California (September 26, 1921), as a result of which two men died. *S.38* (SS-143) sank on July 17, 1923, at Anchorage, Alaska, when its engine room was flooded because a crew member performing routine maintenance removed a valve cover below the waterline.

Right: USS *R.1*, sister ship to *R.6* (SS-83), which suffered a torpedo tube malfunction, September 26, 1921, causing her to sink, with the deaths of two of her crew. She was refloated October 13, 1921, and refitted, serving on until 1946.

Above: USS *S.1*, sister ship to *S.5* (SS-110), shown temporarily being used as an aircraft carrier. *S.5* sank when an experienced crewman was momentarily distracted and then over-compensated for his error. The boat came to rest on the bottom at a depth of 194 feet, but all the crew were eventually rescued.

Left: USS *S.5*'s stern is just clear of the water. Her captain so lightened the after part of the submarine that he brought the stern clear, enabling a hole to be cut. A passing ship saw the flag waving from the hole and called on a Swedish ship for assistance, and the crew was rescued after a very uncomfortable 51 hours in what could so easily have become their coffin.

Another American boat, *S.5* (SS-110), met her fate due to a momentary lapse by an experienced man. Having only recently been commissioned, *S.5* was on final trials when, on September 1, 1920, she made a "crash dive" about fifty miles off Cape May, New Jersey. The petty officer responsible for closing the main air induction valve was distracted at the critical moment and then, realizing his error, grabbed the handle so hard that the valve jammed and water poured into the forward part of the boat, which filled quickly. Within four minutes the boat bottomed at 194 feet.

With little chance of being found, the commanding officer, Captain Charles Cooke, Jr. emptied the main and fuel tanks, which brought the stern up. The battery room had to be sealed to prevent any leakage of chlorine and, with the submarine virtually standing on its bows, the situation was very uncomfortable. Once the submariners were convinced that the stern was clear of the water a hole was cut through the pressure hull, but it was hard going and after thirty-six hours the hole was only some three inches in diameter.

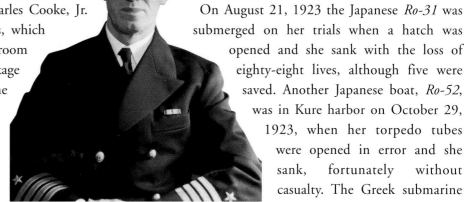

Above: Captain Charles Cooke, Jr. U.S. Navy, whose brilliant improvisation resulted in the rescue of every one of his crew from the sunken submarine *S.5*.

A flag was waved from the hole, attracting the attention of a passing ship, SS *Alanthus*, which lowered a boat and made voice contact with the men inside the submarine. *Alanthus* broadcast an SOS, which brought the Swedish ship, SS *General Goethals*, onto the scene. Realizing that the situation was critical, *General Goethals'* chief engineer managed to pry a large steel plate from the hull, enabling the crew to leave their submarine some fifty-one hours after it had sunk. The first U.S. Navy help arrived the following morning and the battleship USS *Ohio* (BB-12) took the hulk under tow, but the submarine broke loose and sank, never to be recovered.

On August 21, 1923 the Japanese *Ro-31* was submerged on her trials when a hatch was opened and she sank with the loss of eighty-eight lives, although five were saved. Another Japanese boat, *Ro-52*, was in Kure harbor on October 29, 1923, when her torpedo tubes were opened in error and she sank, fortunately without casualty. The Greek submarine *Nereus* was also lost due to a misunderstood order (May 11, 1931); forty-one submariners died, there being no survivors.

Above: French submarine *Prométhée* sank in the English Channel, July 8, 1932, due to an open main ballast tank valve. As often happens when submarines sink, there were extra men aboard, making survival more difficult than with just the normal—and properly trained—crew. Just seven out of 73 escaped.

The Chilean submarine *Rucumilla* was also a victim of error, when, on a training dive, a crewman opened a valve instead of closing it (June 2, 1919). As water poured in, the captain immediately blew the tanks and the bow rose above the water just long enough for a merchant ship lookout to see and report it, resulting in salvage vessels and three cranes being dispatched immediately to the area. The boat was located and raised, but as it reached the surface a chain broke, so it was lowered back to the seabed. Inside the boat conditions were bad: there was no light, water was up to waist level and had reached the batteries, and there were periodic explosions.

As always, everything depended on the commanding officer, Lieutenant Commander del Solar, who kept calm, encouraged his inexperienced crew, and released periodic bursts of compressed air to sweeten the atmosphere. The second lift was totally successful and as soon as the upper deck was clear of the water the hatch was opened and the twenty-five exhausted crewmen aboard emerged safely. The Chilean Navy is renowned for its efficiency and this was a prime example.

On July 8, 1932, the French submarine *Prométhée* sank in the English Channel, following a hydraulic failure that allowed the main ballast tank vents to open. The normal crew was sixty-one, but there were seventy-three men aboard, of whom just seven escaped.

Above: HMS *M.2*, one of many inter-war boats converted to carry aircraft. It is believed her crew were in a rush to launch the aircraft on surfacing and allowed water to flood the interior, taking all 60 of them to their deaths.

During the inter-war period several navies built submarines that carried a small reconnaissance floatplane in a hangar. One such was the British *M.2*, which, on January 26, 1932, carried out a routine dive in Portland Bay, southern England. She disappeared and, after an intensive search, was found eight days later. Divers established that both her hangar door and the hatch between the hangar and the inside of the submarine were open, and it was assumed that the crew had been in too much of a hurry to launch the aircraft on surfacing. Whatever the reason, all sixty aboard died.

NAVIGATION ERRORS

The British submarine *G-11* was the first to be lost after the Armistice (November 11, 1918) when it was wrecked on the Northumberland coast, north-east England, on November 22, 1918, but with the loss of only two lives.

Two American submarines were fortunate. *S.19* (SS-124) was pushed by strong winds and powerful seas onto the southern shore of Cape Cod during the early

Left: USS *S.19* (SS-124) was driven onto Cape Cod, January 13, 1925, in weather so bad it took twelve hours to get a line aboard. Eventually every member of the crew was saved and *S.19* returned to full service.

Right: The torpedo compartment of *S.48*, showing the inboard caps of the four 21-inch torpedo tubes. The entire crew escaped through the top left tube, the very steep angle of the boat giving them very little purchase as they pushed themselves upwards to freedom. (The chains are for moving the torpedoes and reloading the tubes.)

Left: USS *S.48* (SS-159) has the dubious distinction of being involved in two major disasters—first, sinking in Long Island Sound, as seen here, and secondly running aground on the New Hampshire coast, January 25, 1925.

hours of January 13, 1925. The weather was so bad that it took the Coast Guard rescuers some twelve hours to get a line aboard, but they eventually succeeded and all the submarine's crew were saved. The submarine was later recovered and returned to service. Only two weeks later (January 25), *S.48* (SS-159) was off the New Hampshire coast when high winds and heavy snow reduced visibility to zero. At about 1930 she hit the rocks off Jeffrey Point. Her crew refloated her, but she then ran aground again. The crew radioed for help, and

Above: USS *H.1* (SS-28) caught fire off the California coast and was deliberately beached, allowing all but four of the crew to escape, March 12, 1920. The captain, whose decision saved so many lives, was one of those to die.

Coast Guard lifeboats arrived at about 0500, when all the crew were rescued. The hulk was recovered a week later and returned to service for a second time.

H.1 (SS-28) was sailing along the West Coast on March 12, 1920, when a fire broke out while she was off Santa Margareta Island, California. With the fire out of control, her captain deliberately ran her onto the rocks, but he and three others were killed as they tried to reach the shore. The hulk was refloated on March 24, but then sank and was abandoned.

CAUSE UNKNOWN

If finding the hulk of the British *M.2* enabled some guesses to be made as to what might have happened, there were other boats that were never found and their fate remains a mystery. Thus, the British *K.5*, following the dismal record of its class, disappeared in the Bay of Biscay on January 20, 1920, when taking part in an exercise; a few identifiable artifacts—a plank and a sailor's ditty box—were all that was ever found. Similarly, the French *Phenix* disappeared in the South

China Sea on June 15, 1939. Between them these two submarines took 128 men to their deaths.

FOUNDERED

Two boats, one American, one British, foundered. USS *Tuna* (SS-27) was used mainly for experimental work and was decommissioned in April 1919, following which she was used as a target for various weapons systems. On July 30, 1919, she was being inspected by a six-man team when she sank without warning, taking three of the inspectors with her. The reason for this apparently avoidable tragedy was never established. The loss of the British *L.9* was easier to understand; she was at anchor in Hong Kong harbor on August 18, 1923, when the place was hit by a typhoon. The submarine sank, without loss of life, and was later recovered and returned to service.

SANK AT MOORINGS

The British *K.15*'s end was less dramatic than that of some of her fellows. On the early evening of June 25, 1921, she was lying alongside a cruiser with most of her crew ashore. The officer of the day suddenly realized that she was sinking and the few men aboard abandoned ship immediately—nobody wasted any time leaving a threatened K-boat! She sank minutes later and the loss was later attributed to the hot weather having caused a hydraulic leak, allowing the vents to open slightly.

COLLISIONS

By far the largest number of casualties during the inter-war period were due to collisions: nine each with merchant ships and warships; four with other submarines; and one unknown. In total, these collisions involved the loss of no fewer than 658 lives. As in the previous periods, this was primarily because submarines' lights were difficult to see, and the boats were small and vulnerable compared to merchant ships; the result was that they invariably suffered far more. Three were lost with all hands.

The Italian submarine *Veniero* disappeared off Cape Passero, Sicily, on August 6, 1925, and heavy scars were

Left: Submarine HMS *M.1*, armed with a 12-inch gun, was one of many inter-war boats sunk in a surface collision, in her case with a merchant ship, November 12, 1925. She was the largest submarine of the day, but the British boat simply rolled over and sank with all hands.

Below: USS *O.5* (SS-66) was sunk in a collision at the entrance to the Panama Canal, October 28, 1923, her loss being accompanied by an act of exceptional bravery by one of her crew.

subsequently found on the hull of the merchant ship SS *Capena*, indicating that she had probably been responsible. On September 25 that year the American *S.51* (SS-162) was sailing off Block Island, when she was hit by the Italian liner *City of Rome*, which cut a huge hole in the submarine's side and then rode over her. An unknown number of submariners escaped into the icy waters, but only three survived. The British *M.1*, a huge monitor fitted with a 12-inch gun, was one of the largest submarines of her day, but that did not save her when she was hit by a merchant ship. She was lost, with all hands, on November 12, 1925.

Collisions with merchant ships also caused the loss of the French *Ondine* (October 3, 1928) and Russian *L.55* (October 24, 1931), both with all hands, while on June 9, 1931, the British *Poseidon* collided with a merchant ship in the South China Sea, but thirty-five men were saved out of a crew of fifty-seven.

The sinking of the American submarine *O.5* (SS-66) in a collision on October 28, 1923, was accompanied by an act of exceptional bravery. The boat was about to transit the Panama Canal when it was hit by SS *Abangarez* and

Above: Torpedoman Henry Breault of USS *O.5* receives the Congressional Medal of Honor from President Coolidge, March 8, 1924. Breault voluntarily returned to the sinking boat to rescue a friend, went down with it, and kept his friend alive until rescued 31 hours later.

sank within a minute. Sixteen men escaped immediately and three were killed, but Torpedoman Henry Breault was about to leave the sinking submarine when he noticed that a comrade was missing. He returned to the torpedo room and found his friend, but then realized that the only way to save him was to lock the torpedo room hatch from the inside, which he did. The boat then sank and the two men remained trapped until the boat was recovered by a salvage team some thirty-one hours later. Breault was awarded a richly deserved Medal of Honor.

COLLISIONS WITH WARSHIPS

Collisions with warships also took a heavy toll of boats and men, almost invariably with no survivors. The British *H.42* was hit by a destroyer, HMS *Versatile* (March 23, 1922—twenty-six lost), and *L.24* off Portland Bill by the battleship HMS *Resolution* (January 10, 1924—forty-three lost).

Similarly, Japanese *Ro-25* was hit by a cruiser (March 19, 1924—forty-six dead), the Italian *F.14* by a destroyer (August 6, 1928—twenty-seven dead), and the Soviet *Tovarich* by battleship *Murat* (July 23, 1935—fifty-five dead). Somewhat more fortunate was Germany's brand-new *U-18*, which was hit by a tender (November 20, 1936), but in this case twelve of the twenty-man crew escaped.

COLLISIONS WITH SUBMARINES

Collisions between submarines invariably took place during training. The British *H.47* and *L.12* collided on July 9, 1929, with the loss of twenty-one from *H.47* and three from *L.12*, but both made it back to port. When the Japanese *I-63* and *I-60* collided, however, the former sank with the loss of eighty-one lives (six survived), while the Russian *Rabotchi* collided with an unnamed submarine in the Baltic (May 22, 1931) and was lost with all thirty-nine of her crew.

DISASTER AVERTED

USS *R.14* (SS-91) avoided a potential disaster in considerable style. In May 1921 the submarine, based on Pearl Harbor, took part in a search for a missing tugboat. Due to a miscalculation, she ran out of fuel when some 250 miles from base, a most unusual occurrence. The boat lacked a wireless and, rather than wait to be found, which might have taken some time, the crew set to and sewed sheets and mattress covers together to produce makeshift sails. Then, using the periscopes as masts, the crew sailed *R-14* home, arriving on May 15, 1921.

Right: In May 1921, USS *R.14* (SS-91) ran out of fuel some 250 miles off Hawaii while searching for a missing ship. Without a wireless, but certainly not lacking in imagination and initiative, the crew sewed sheets and mattress covers together and sailed her home!

Above: Italian submarine *F.14* was sunk in a collision with the Italian destroyer *Missori*, August 6, 1928; all 27 of the submarine's crew were lost.

Right: The bows of the British destroyer HMS *Versatile* after colliding with submarine HMS *H.42* off Gibraltar, March 23, 1922. All 27 aboard the submarine died.

Above: British submarine *H.41* was sunk while lying alongside her depot ship, October 18, 1919, when destroyer HMS *Vulcan* came too close and holed the submarine's hull. *H.41* was raised but never returned to service.

USS SQUALUS (SS-192)

CLASS: Sargo.

DISPLACEMENT: submerged 2,350 tons.

DIMENSIONS: length 310 feet, beam 27 feet.

PROPULSION: diesel-electric.

PERFORMANCE: surface 20 knots, submerged 9 knots; diving depth 250 feet.

ARMAMENT: 8 x 21-inch torpedo tubes (20 torpedoes); 1 x 3-inch gun.

CREW: 55.

The U.S. Navy submarine *Squalus* (SS-192) sank at 0845 on May 23, 1939, while on a crash-dive trial with fifty-nine aboard (crew plus officials). A valve had been left open, although the indicator showed it to be shut. As the engine room flooded, the watertight door was closed and twenty-six men inside died immediately. The submarine bottomed at 242 feet, with thirty-three men still alive.

Squalus's failure to surface was quickly noticed and another submarine, *Sculpin*, found the telephone buoy; the two captains spoke, but the line then broke. Meanwhile, the rescue ship *Falcon* carrying the McCann Rescue Chamber reached the site at about 0430. After six hours of unrelenting work *Falcon* was moored over *Squalus* and a diver found the submarine and secured the downhaul shackle to the escape hatch bolt.

Commander A. R. McCann, designer of the rescue chamber, took charge of operations and the bell soon mated with the submarine, where, having equalized the pressures, the submarine hatch was opened, some twenty-eight hours after it had sunk. The foul air was vented and fresh air piped in, following which the first seven men were taken to the surface, followed by two lifts of nine and a last of eight. That final lift was fraught with peril as a cable snagged and the chamber had to be lowered back to the submarine so that it could be cleared. The final party reached the rescue ship at 0030, more than thirty-nine hours after their boat had sunk.

Left: Invented in the United States, the McCann Rescue Chamber proved a great success and was also operated by the British Royal Navy, as seen here.

Above: *Squalus's* bow comes into sight in the struggle to refloat her and recover the bodies of the 26 men who had died in the tragedy, May 23, 1939.

Right: Anxious men watch from the decks of the rescue ship *Falcon* as the McCann Rescue Chamber floats alongside. The chamber successfully rescued all 33 men who survived *Squalus's* initial sinking, which was due to a faulty valve.

HMS THETIS

DISPLACEMENT: submerged 1,573 tons.

DIMENSIONS: length 275 feet, beam 26 feet.

PROPULSION: diesel-electric.

PERFORMANCE: surface 15 knots, submerged 9 knots; diving depth 300 feet.

ARMAMENT: 10 x 21-inch torpedo tubes (16 torpedoes); 1 x 4-inch gun.

CREW: 53.

Left: *Thetis* was a brand-new boat on her first diving trial when she sank due to a combination of errors, with no fewer than 103 people aboard; only four survived.

Below: The margin between success and failure was very small; despite the stern initially being out of the water *Thetis* eventually sank to the bottom.

The British submarine *Thetis*, a brand-new boat, sank on June 1, 1939, on her first diving trial, with both her crew and numerous dockyard hands, a total of 103 people, aboard. The trial commenced at 1356, but observers aboard the escorting tug saw that the submarine submerged extremely slowly, until, at 1458, she suddenly disappeared from view.

The initial problem was due to an incorrect trim calculation, but her sudden dive was due to a misunderstanding over No5 torpedo tube; the outboard end was open and, when the inboard end was also opened, the forward part of the boat flooded, taking her to the bottom.

It was several hours before the alarm was raised and then, through a combination of errors, the submarine was not found until 0730 the following morning, when the destroyer *Brazen* discovered some eighteen feet of her stern sticking out of the water. By chance, the first two survivors made a successful

Right: *Thetis*'s main problem occurred when both outer and inner torpedo tube doors were opened simultaneously: as a result every door in every submarine was modified to prevent this from happening again.

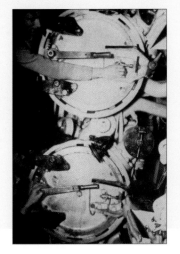

escape as *Brazen* arrived and described what had happened and what was required to rescue those below.

In the submarine the situation was serious. Repeated attempts to expel the water from the forward end had failed, while the large number of men in a reduced space were consuming the oxygen and exhaling harmful carbon dioxide. Further, the small amount of emergency food aboard was in the flooded bow compartment. Following the first two escapes no further attempts were made until about 0900 when four men entered the submarine's escape chamber, but there was a problem and the chamber had to be drained down, when three were found to be dead and the fourth dying. However, two men made a further escape attempt at 1000, and were successful; they were the last to leave alive.

Those on the surface made frantic plans to gain access to the submarine, including opening a series of manhole covers and cutting through the hull with an oxyacetylene torch. A wire was passed around the stern but this broke after several hours and the stricken submarine sank to the bottom.

Ashore, frantic efforts were being made to assemble the right men and the equipment for the rescue operation, but this took time. Some divers came from Scapa Flow, but arrived without their equipment and had to borrow some on arrival. Attempts were also made to secure pontoons and lift *Thetis* to the surface, but all to no avail. At 1610, some forty-eight hours after the submarine had dived, it was officially declared that all hope of rescuing the remaining submariners had been abandoned.

PART III: 1939-1945

Left: World War Two saw the most intense submarine campaigns ever fought, but, as in World War One, by no means all the losses were the result of enemy action. Boats continued to be lost through collisions, bad weather, and human error, and even the largest submarine of its day, the French *Surcouf*, which displaced 4,304 tons, was not immune, disappearing in the Caribbean in February 1942, probably as the result of a collision.

PART III: 1939-1945

World War Two saw a major expansion in the submarine fleets of the major belligerents, principally the United States, United Kingdom, Soviet Union, Germany and Japan. All navies lost large numbers of men and submarines due to enemy action, but losses due to the hazards of the sea, errors, miscalculations and mechanical defects were also considerable.

OPERATIONAL LOSS; CAUSE UNKNOWN		
COUNTRY	**BOATS LOST**	**MEN DIED**
Italy	4	166
Japan	14	1,297
Germany	48	2,490
France	1	159
UK	2	59
USA	7	460
TOTAL	76	4,631

During the course of World War Two six belligerent navies lost seventy-six submarines to unknown causes, taking 4,631 men to their deaths—see table. For many of these, their disappearance cannot be pinned down to a specific date, but simply to the date of sailing or, in some cases, to some time following the last radio transmission. The terms "diving accident" or "possible mine" are sometimes applied, but the fact is that these are just guesses and nobody knows the real causes.

The German Hartherz group of submarines, for example, assembled in the Atlantic on February 4, 1943, and included *U-519*, which was still with the group when it dispersed on the 8th, but nothing was ever heard from it again. USS *Escolar* (SS-294), a Balao-class boat, was one of seven U.S. Navy submarines lost to unknown causes and her story is very similar. She was operating in the Yellow Sea on September 30, 1944, when she reported by radio that she was in action with a Japanese gunboat, but appears to have been unharmed, as she later made several routine

Right: Turkish submarine *Atilay* disappeared on July 14, 1942, an event usually attributed to a "diving accident." But she was modern and well built, and the Turkish Navy had long experience of submarine operations, thus the reality is that nobody knows what caused the loss.

contacts with both USS *Croaker* (SS-246) and USS *Perch* (SS-313). *Escolar*'s last known transmission was received by *Perch* on October 17, following which—nothing. *Escolar* failed to arrive at Midway on November 13, as scheduled, and was declared missing two weeks later. Postwar examination of Allied records with regard to the loss of *U-519* and to Japanese records for *Escolar* reveal no attacks that might explain either of these two disappearances, and there were no known minefields anywhere near them. So, whether these losses were due to some unrecorded enemy action, the hazards of the sea, or some error on the part of a crew member will never be known.

U-503, a German Type VIIC, sailed from Stavanger, Norway, on February 15, 1945, to engage in deep diving trials. She was expected to return the same day, but failed to do so. Similarly, USS *O.9* (SS-70) was undertaking deep diving trials off the Isle of Shoals (June 20, 1941) when she failed to surface. In this case, the hulk was located, lying at a depth of some 400 feet, and while some courageous

Right: Rueful smiles on the bridge of German *U-957*, as she returns from a training exercise during which she collided with a tender, the angle of the periscope mute witness to the force of the impact. The German submarine training organization in the Baltic had a very poor record for such accidents, many of which, unlike this one, resulted in loss of life, as well as of U-boats.

Left: The German Navy was the first to develop the snorkel tube into an operational device, as seen here on *U-855*, a Type IXC/40. In the early days several boats disappeared without trace, possibly due to faults in the snorkel itself or to incorrect use by an inexperienced crew.

divers managed to reach her for necessarily brief visits it was decided that there was no chance that anyone remained alive and that further recovery work was too hazardous, so she was abandoned. Clearly both *U-503* and *O.9* were crushed by exceeding their permitted maximum depths, but the reason why they did so will never be established.

Sometimes there is collateral evidence to suggest a cause, as in the case of *U-865*, a German Type IXC-40, which disappeared in September 1944. She was fitted with the then very new snorkel tube, which enabled her to recharge her batteries while running submerged, and this was known to have given her constant trouble, forcing her to return to port no fewer than three times for repairs, before departing on her final voyage. This suggests that a malfunctioning snorkel may have played a role in her eventual disappearance.

In another case, in early May 1945 USS *Baya* (SS-318) and *Lagarto* (SS-371) were ordered to operate in the Gulf of Siam. On the night of May 2/3 *Baya* conducted a solo attack on a tanker, but was driven off by the radar-equipped Japanese escorts, and the two American submarines met the following morning so that their officers could discuss their plans for a coordinated surface attack that night (May 3/4). As agreed, *Baya* tried to attack at midnight only to be driven off yet again, but the following morning when she tried to contact *Lagarto* there

was no reply. In a postwar examination of Japanese records it was discovered that the destroyer escort *Hatsutaka* had carried out an antisubmarine attack that night and in that area, so it seems a reasonable deduction that the target could well have been *Lagarto*, which is therefore presumed to have sunk with all hands.

A more puzzling episode involved USS *R.12* (SS-89) which, on June 12, 1943, was on a training mission off Key West, Florida, and running on the surface preparatory to diving to undertake a torpedo approach against a simulated target. The boat was ready to dive, with the commanding officer about to leave the bridge, when the collision alarm was activated from below, and a brief message was received topsides that the forward battery compartment was flooding. The commanding officer immediately gave orders to blow the main ballast tanks and close all hatches, but he was too late and the submarine sank underneath him within some fifteen seconds of the alarm having been sounded. The commanding officer and five other watchkeepers on the bridge survived, but forty-two men (including two Brazilian Navy observers) died. The hull came to rest in some 600 feet of water, far too deep for any recovery attempts. A subsequent Court of Inquiry concluded that, while the loss of *R.12* was clearly due to flooding, the reason for this would never be established. It was suggested that one possibility was that both outboard and inboard doors on one of the torpedo tubes might have been opened simultaneously, but obviously this could never be proved.

The Imperial Japanese Navy lost fourteen submarines and 1,297 men to unknown causes, the proportionally greater number of casualties being due to

Above: The Japanese suffered a large number of "operational losses" of submarines and men during the war. One such was *I-22*, which failed to return from a mission in October 1942, but none of the U.S. forces claimed her sinking.

Left: When World War Two started in 1939, the Italian Navy had the world's largest submarine fleet, many of its boats being of very modern construction, such as the *Squalo*, seen here. The Italians lost four of these boats and 166 men to unknown causes in the following four years.

the much larger crews in Japanese submarines. *I.67* disappeared in August 1940, when her country was still technically at peace, with the loss of eighty-nine lives, and *I.33* was on sea trials when she disappeared, but the others were all on operations. Many unsolved cases remain, of which forty-eight are German, and some of these would undoubtedly have been due to Allied antisubmarine attacks, but what proportion is simply not known.

COLLISIONS WITH SURFACE SHIPS

There were eighteen collisions between submarines and surface ships during the period, eleven of them involving German U-boats. Of those, seven took place in the Baltic during training exercises. The British suffered two such collisions, the USA, Italy and Netherlands one each, and even neutral Sweden suffered two.

COLLISIONS WITH OTHER SUBMARINES

No fewer than eleven German U-boats were involved in submarine-on-submarine collisions, nine of them in the Baltic in training. The only other navy to suffer such a

Above: Italian Settembrini-class submarine *Ruggiero Settimo*. During the war, the Italian Navy operated in the Mediterranean Sea, as well as the Atlantic and Indian Oceans.

Above: Despite being neutral, the Swedish Navy lost several submarines during the war, including the *Sjöborren*, which collided with a merchant ship in the Baltic on September 4, 1942, but with the loss of only one life.

disaster was Japan, where *Ro-62* hit *Ro-66*, with only three men from the latter surviving out of a crew of fifty-nine. The most costly collision to befall German U-boats took place during a wolf-pack surface attack on a convoy of British tank-landing craft off Cape Finisterre in the early hours of May 4, 1943. Although this took place during a combat operation, there was no involvement by the enemy. Two of the boats, *U-439* and *U-659*, were heading towards the convoy when one of the targets blew up in a spectacular explosion and it would appear that this may have distracted the submarine lookouts, who failed to realize how close the two U-boats were to each other. At this point, the captain of *U-439* came onto the bridge and ordered a turn to port, resulting, almost immediately, in a collision with *U-659*. The latter sank at once, leaving just a few watchkeepers struggling on the surface, while *U-439* went full astern to disengage from its victim. Unfortunately, this coincided with a large following wave sweeping over the boat, flooding the diesel exhausts, which stopped the engines; the boat then flooded and sank. Some time later a British vessel spotted lifebuoy lights in the water and picked up twelve survivors from the two German boats, meaning that eighty-four men died from this combination of errors.

Another collision had fatal consequences when *U-254* and *U-221*, both submerged, collided with each other during an attack on a convoy (December 8, 1942). *U-254* was badly damaged, managed to surface, but could not dive again. She was then unable to take evasive action when attacked by an RAF Liberator and was sunk; forty-one crewmen died, but four were saved by *U-221*.

Above: Swedish submarine *Illern* (picture shows sister-ship *Uttern*) also collided with a merchant ship, with the loss of one life, August 12, 1943.

Below: Early Type VIIAs prepare for an inspection in the late 1930s. The German Navy had to create a submarine force, virtually from scratch, from 1936 onwards and there were a number of accidents due to inexperience and over-enthusiasm.

SUNK ALONGSIDE

Even with the heightened awareness resulting from being at war, navies continued to suffer from sinkings in dock. The Germans lost two boats in this way: *U-43* at Lorient, France (December 17, 1943—see box), and *U-28* at Neustadt in German waters (March 17, 1944). The Italians lost *Zoea* at Taranto in 1942, and the United States *Lancetfish* (SS-296) at Boston (March 17, 1945).

HAZARDS OF THE SEA

The hazards of the sea were just as relentless in wartime as in peace, with submarines being wrecked, running aground or foundering in storms. The U.S. Navy lost four submarines to such causes. *S.36* (SS-141) and *S.39* (SS-144) were wrecked, while *S.27* (SS-132) and *Darter* (SS-227) ran aground, but with no loss of life.

Above: USS *Peto* (SS-265), one of the US Navy's Gato-class. A few of these boats operated in the Atlantic, but most were in the Pacific, where they took the war to the very shores of Japan. They were strong, well-designed and with many safety aids, but even so a number disappeared without trace and without any entries in Japanese logs that might offer an explanation.

SURCOUF

DISPLACEMENT: submerged 4,304 tons.	
DIMENSIONS: length 361 feet, beam 30 feet.	
PROPULSION: diesel-electric.	
PERFORMANCE: surface 19 knots, submerged 10 knots; diving depth 262 feet.	
ARMAMENT: 12 x 21.7-inch torpedo tubes (14 torpedoes); 2 x 8-inch, 2 x 37mm guns.	
CREW: 118.	

Above: *Surcouf*, showing her twin 8-inch guns, designed to enable her to engage enemy surface ships, such as destroyers, a requirement which never once arose.

Completed in 1935, the French submarine *Surcouf* was the largest submarine of her day, having been designed as a commerce raider with a global range. For this, she was armed with two 8-inch guns, carried a scouting aircraft, and even had accommodation for forty prisoners! During World War Two she was employed in the Caribbean, but following Pearl Harbor it was decided to send her to Tahiti to help defend French Pacific territories.

Below: *Surcouf* being refitted in dry dock. As large as a destroyer, she disappeared without trace on February 18, 1942, taking her crew and 41 other men with her.

Having victualed for this long voyage at the U.S. submarine base at New London she set sail for the Panama Canal. She never arrived and it is accepted by most people that she was run down by the U.S. merchant ship *Thomas Lykes* on the night of February 18, 1942. However, there have been persistent, albeit totally unproven, rumors that she was seen replenishing German U-boats and was then sunk by the Americans. Whatever the truth, she disappeared and the loss of 159 lives makes this the greatest single submarine disaster.

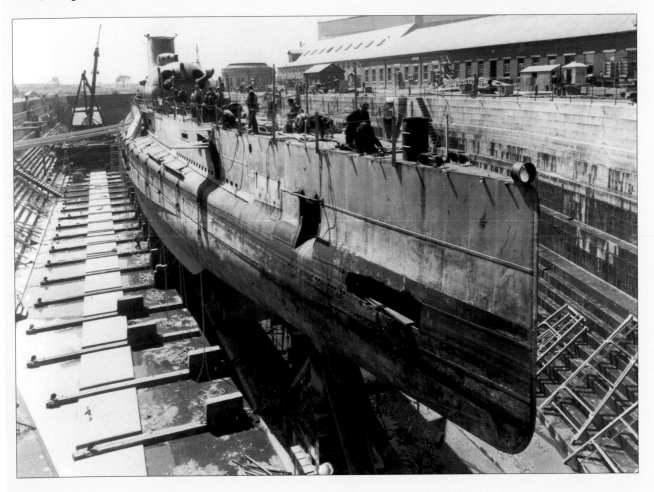

HMS UNTAMED

| DISPLACEMENT: submerged 740 tons. |
| DIMENSIONS: length 197 feet, beam 16 feet. |
| PROPULSION: diesel-electric. |
| PERFORMANCE: surface 11 knots, submerged 9 knots; diving depth 200 feet. |
| ARMAMENT: 4 x 21-inch torpedo tubes (8 torpedoes); 1 x 3-inch gun. |
| CREW: 33. |

The British submarine HMS *Untamed* had been commissioned just under two months, when, on May 30, 1943, she was serving as an antisubmarine target. The weather was fine, the sea smooth. *Untamed* was submerged when the distance-measuring log ceased to operate. The repair drill was to withdraw the log into its tube, close the tube-end valve and bring the log into the hull for repair, but when this was done water gushed into the boat; the valve was wrongly connected. The watertight door was closed but the weight of water took the boat to the bottom. All efforts to surface having failed, the captain ordered abandon ship via the engine-room escape hatch. With the crew ready, the flooding valve was opened, but no water entered; this valve, too, was incorrectly connected. Attempts to admit water via another valve proved so slow that the air became very contaminated, forcing the crew to don their escape masks. However, all died from oxygen poisoning. The boat was raised and returned to service as HMS *Vitality*.

This unnecessary loss was due to a combination of factors, primarily the faulty valves and poor quality assurance in the yard, although the newness of the crew may have played a part.

Right: HMS *Untamed*, a brand-new boat, was lost in May 1943, due to a combination of totally avoidable errors made during construction.

GERMAN NAVY TRAINING LOSSES: 1935-45

	SCHOOL BOAT	WORKING UP	TOTALS
COLLISION; SURFACE SHIP	4	5	9
COLLISION; U-BOAT	0	10	10
DIVING ACCIDENT	3	2	5
SANK ALONGSIDE	1	0	1
TOTALS	8	17	25

In the period 1935-45 the German U-boat arm lost a total of twenty-five submarines and 549 men killed in training accidents, a loss rate unparalleled in any other navy and which was achieved without any involvement by Germany's enemies. The sea training system involved two elements. First was individual training, where aspiring U-boatmen put into practice skills learned in the classroom, such as submarine seamanship, engineering, maintenance, navigation and gunnery. These practical lessons took place aboard "school boats," which were permanently allocated to the training organization.

The second element involved the working-up of newly commissioned crews to produce an efficient team, capable of meeting whatever the Allies threw at them from the moment they started their first operational voyage.

Surprisingly, nineteen of the losses were the result of collisions with other vessels involved in the training program. Nine of these involved surface ships and it is surprising that the safety rules did not prevent this. Another ten of the losses were in collisions between U-boats in the working up program.

It is a truism that the harder men train for war the easier the actual operations will be, and the U-boat arm certainly trained its men hard. But the German Navy was desperately short of U-boats and crews, and it is astonishing that they accepted such a high loss rate.

Left: *U-2332*, a German Type XXIII. One of two new types entering service in 1944-5, it required a great deal of training to handle properly.

Above: *U-18* entered service in January 1936 when the U-boat service was working-up, and was sunk in a collision with a surface ship, November 20, 1936; 8 died, 12 survived. She was raised, returned to service, and operated throughout World War Two.

FRIENDLY FIRE (HMS P.514)

DISPLACEMENT: submerged 680 tons.

DIMENSIONS: length 186 feet, beam 18 feet.

PROPULSION: diesel-electric.

PERFORMANCE: surface 14 knots, submerged 11 knots; diving depth 200 feet.

ARMAMENT: 4 x 21-inch torpedo tubes (8 torpedoes); 1 x 3-inch gun.

CREW: 33.

All services and all nations suffer from "friendly fire." These are incidents where death or destruction is meted out in error on friendly ships, troops or aircraft. The modern term is "blue-on-blue" and all are tragedies. Submarines seem particularly susceptible to such incidents; one example among many was HMS *P.514*.

Built as USS *R.19*, this boat served in the U.S. Navy for twenty-four years before being transferred to the Royal Navy in March 1942. Only three months later she was sailing from Argentina to St Johns, Newfoundland, when at 0300 on June 21, 1942, she was spotted on the surface by Canadian minesweeper HMCS *Georgian*. The Canadian ship signaled the challenge of the day, to which there was no reply, and assuming very reasonably that it was an enemy U-boat, *Georgian* ran in and rammed. It was a most efficient attack and *P.514* sank immediately; there were no survivors.

An official enquiry found that *Georgian*'s captain had acted in good faith, since his challenge had gone unanswered. Sadly, there was nobody from *P.514* to explain why.

Above: In another example of a probable "blue-on-blue" incident, Dutch submarine *O.13* disappeared in June 1940 on a war patrol. It is thought to have been in a collision with Polish submarine *Wilk*, which was operating in the same area.

Right: In a disastrous friendly fire "own goal" USS *Tullibee* (SS-284) sank with all hands except Gunner's Mate Kuykendall, while attacking a Japanese convoy, March 14, 1944. He reported that *Tullibee* was hit by her own torpedo, a freak accident that has happened to several submarines in both war and peace. Picture shows *Perch* (SS-313), identical sister to *Tullibee*.

SUNK ALONGSIDE

CLASS: Type IXA.

DISPLACEMENT: submerged 1,153 tons.

DIMENSIONS: length 251 feet, beam 21 feet.

PROPULSION: diesel-electric.

PERFORMANCE: surface 18 knots, submerged 8 knots; diving depth 755 feet.

ARMAMENT: 6 x 21-inch torpedo tubes (22 torpedoes); 1 x 105mm, 1 x 30mm guns.

CREW: 48.

Twenty-one submarines have sunk when lying alongside, almost invariably due to human negligence. The boats were then raised without much difficulty and most returned to service, but only after an absence from the operational fleet for several months.

A prime example occurred on February 3/4, 1941, at Lorient, France, where *U-43*, a Type IXA, was due to sail at dawn. Kapitänleutnant Lüth was an experienced commanding officer, who, following final preparations for sailing, sent most of the crew ashore for a night "on the town," leaving a guard of a petty officer and six sailors, all new to submarines. Unfortunately, someone had left a valve slightly open—whether deliberately or accidentally was never established—and the boat started to sink slowly and imperceptibly, but maintaining an even keel. By the time anybody noticed what was happening it was too late and the problem was compounded by the fact that the watertight doors were left open, contrary to standing orders; the end result was that the boat sank until only the top of the bridge was visible.

Lüth was reprimanded by Admiral Dönitz and half the crew were set to clean the boat, while the other half were sent for re-training. *U-43* was out of service for three months.

PART IV: 1945-1975

Left: Following World War Two, the most significant technological innovation was nuclear propulsion, which made submarines truly independent of the surface and gave them speed, endurance, operating depths, size and habitability which had hitherto only been dreamt of. There were also hazards, as discovered by USS *Thresher* (SSN-593) when she disappeared April 19, 1963, while on post-refit trials with the loss of 129 lives. Seen here is sister-ship, USS *Haddock* (SSN-621).

PART IV: 1945-1975

The Cold War started in 1947 and the ever-present threat of global nuclear conflict had a major influence on submarine numbers, capabilities and deployments. But the most significant development of all was the introduction in the 1950s of nuclear propulsion and nuclear-armed weapons, resulting in a quantum jump in performance and capability, but also introducing the potential for a major catastrophe should the propulsion system be damaged in an accident.

COLLISIONS

During the period of the Cold War there was a continuation of the old bugbear of collisions between submarines and surface ships, usually with dire consequences for the submarine and its crew. Spain's worst ever submarine disaster took place off the Balearic Islands on June 27, 1946, when the destroyer *Lepanto* collided with submarine *C.4*, which then sank with the loss of all forty-six crew.

Collisions with merchant ships also continued to claim lives. In January 1950 the British submarine *Truculent* was hit by the Swedish tanker *Divina* and sank with the loss of sixty-four men—see box. In early April 1953 the Turkish submarine *Dumlupinar* was hit by the Swedish vessel *Naboland* and sank in the Dardanelles

Above: Turkish submarine *Dumlupinar*, ex-US Navy *Blower* (SS-325), was hit by a merchant ship while transiting the Dardanelles and sank very quickly. Of her crew, 81 died and five were saved, four of whom had been on the bridge at the time of the collision.

Right: The scene immediately following the collision between destroyer USS *Silverstein* (DE-534) and submarine USS *Stickleback* (SS-415) off Hawaii, May 29, 1958. The destroyer captain is deliberately keeping his ship hard against the submarine to prevent the latter from rolling over and sinking. No lives were lost.

with the loss of eighty-one lives. On June 13, 1973, a Soviet Echo II, *K-56*, collided with the research ship *Akademik Berg*, also Soviet, in what must have been a very serious incident, since twenty-seven of the submarine's crew were killed.

The margin by which disaster is avoided is sometimes a very narrow one. The French *Laubie*, for example, an ex-German Type VIIC, collided with the French ferry *Ville de Marseilles II* on May 2, 1960, but although the boat was seriously damaged, there were no casualties.

In an incident in the Pacific a U.S. Navy crew escaped disaster very narrowly not just once, but twice, in a matter of minutes. The World War Two-era USS

Stickleback (SS-415) was operating as an ASW target for a destroyer-escort, USS *Silverstein* (DE-534), off Pearl Harbor on May 29, 1958. In the final evolution of the day, *Stickleback* was carrying out a simulated submerged torpedo attack when she suddenly lost all power and started to dive steeply. Why this happened has not been explained, but the captain took decisive and successful corrective action, which resulted in the boat reaching the surface. Unfortunately, she was then lying directly in the path of the approaching *Silverstein.* The destroyer, traveling at some speed, could not avoid hitting the submarine at right angles, driving a large hole in her side, just forward of the conning tower. Fortunately, *Silverstein's* commanding officer had the sense

Left: Soviet Navy Hotel III nuclear-powered ballistic missile submarine in distress. Many of the Soviet Navy's first-generation nuclear submarines suffered reactor-related problems, causing many casualties among the crews, but, because of the Soviet secrecy laws, the total human cost may never be established.

to hold his ship in the breach in order to maintain the stricken submarine in an upright position, thus enabling the submarine's crew to reach the upper deck and then to abandon ship in an orderly manner. Thus, after just a few minutes swimming, they were all duly picked up by waiting ships.

The Cold War introduced a new peacetime hazard as the demands of the rival intelligence staffs required NATO and Soviet submarines to approach each other closely to determine what the other was up to and to obtain details of underwater profile, propulsion system, and so on. In such a cat-and-mouse game it was inevitable that errors should be made and there were several collisions, although usually without loss of life.

One of the first to be publicly acknowledged took place on November 15, 1969, in the Barents Sea, when the Soviet Hotel-class submarine *K-19* smashed into the American Scorpion-class USS *Gato* (SSN-615). They were at a depth of some 200 feet and it is clear that it was the Russian sub that hit the American, since *K-19* suffered major damage around her bows. Her sonar was completely destroyed and the covers of the torpedo tubes were deformed. *K-19* surfaced and was able to return to port for repairs, but *Gato* continued with her patrol.

Some six months later (June 20, 1970) there was a second collision between two nuclear-powered submarines, this time in the Pacific. USS *Tautog* (SSN-639) was shadowing Echo II *K-557* when the Soviet captain, suspecting that he was being followed, performed what the Americans described as the "Crazy Ivan" maneuver— i.e., reversing course without warning in order to take the possible tracker by surprise. In this case the Soviet captain was all too successful as his Echo-II slid across the top of *Tautog*, doing considerable damage to both boats. The Americans initially believed that the Russian boat had sunk, but, in fact, both made it back to base.

CAUSE UNKNOWN

The dreaded term "cause unknown" continued to be applicable to submarine disasters. The French suffered no fewer than four serious losses between 1946 and 1970. The first such incident involved the former *U-2366*, a captured German Type XXIII, which was lost off Toulon on December 5, 1946. As the official death toll was twenty-six and the normal crew was fourteen, she must have been seriously overcrowded, although whether this played any part in her loss has never been admitted.

The next loss was *Sibylle*, one of four British S-class boats lent to France by the Royal Navy in 1951. *Sibylle* was at sea in the Mediterranean on September 23, 1952, when she simply disappeared, with her crew of forty-four. No explanation has ever been found. Some fifty S-class Group III boats similar to *Sibylle* were

built, of which only one other, *Stonehenge*, was lost without trace (March 16, 1944), so why *Sibylle* should have gone is a mystery.

Having re-created their submarine design and production capability from virtually zero in 1945 the French built two successful classes in the 1950s which led into the Daphne-class. This entered service in the 1960s. The type proved to be popular in the export market, so that the French were understandably very concerned when *Minerve* disappeared without trace in January 1968, followed by *Eurydice* in March 1970. No reason for these losses could be found, but then, in 1971, another Daphne-class boat, *Flore*, was proceeding submerged when the snorkel sprang a leak, but the alert captain took immediate action and saved his boat. Modification to the others cured the problem, which has never recurred, and for once the designation "cause unknown" could be modified to "probable snorkel problem," but 109 lives had been lost in those two boats.

Between 1958 and 1968 the fledgling Israeli Navy acquired five submarines from the UK, of which the fourth was *Dakar*, the former HMS *Totem*. She was modernized and refitted prior to handing over and sailed for her new home under an Israeli crew on January 9, 1968. She made good progress and sent regular radio reports, but the one sent at 0002 on January 15, when just 360 miles from home, proved to

Above: After a very active war as part of the Free French Navy, *Minerve* had the misfortune to run aground on August 19, 1945. She was thirteen years old and worn out, so she was scrapped rather than rebuilt.

Above: A British T-class submarine, similar to the Israeli *Dakar*, which disappeared in the Mediterranean in 1968. *Dakar's* wreck was found in 1999 and it was discovered that a small leak had led to a fatal loss of trim and then to a dive from which recovery was impossible.

be her last. A series of intensive searches over many years failed to locate her and she continued to be labeled "operational loss; cause unknown." Eventually, however, the wreck was found on May 8, 1999, lying at a depth of some 9,800 feet and broken into several parts. Examination of the wreckage showed that the accident happened when *Dakar* was snorkeling on course for Haifa when, at some time between 0001 and 0300 on January 25, 1968, a relatively minor leak caused the boat to lose her trim, as a result of which she dived suddenly. The captain was unable to take corrective action and she plunged to destruction.

The other two major losses, cause unknown, were the U.S. Navy submarines *Thresher* and *Scorpion*—see boxes.

SUNK IN DOCK

Despite all the technological advances and ever-increasing safety features, two submarines sank in dock during this period—there was no loss of life, but considerable expense was incurred in raising and refitting them. USS *Guitarro* (SSN-665) sank during final fitting out at its builders, the Mare Island Naval Yard. Tests were being made on various tanks, but crucially various hatches were open, some of them carrying cables which meant that they could not be closed, while inside the submarine the entrance hatch to the sonar compartment (and its protective coffer dam) had both been removed and stored carefully—ashore. There were also failures of command and control in the dockyard organization, which meant that warnings of impending calamity were not heeded. The Congressional investigation pulled no punches: "The *Guitarro* should not have sunk. It was not overwhelmed by cataclysmic forces of nature or an imperfection in design or an inherent weakness in its hull. Rather, it was sent to the bottom by the action, or inaction, of certain construction workers who either failed

to recognize an actual or potential threat to the ship's safety or assumed that it was not their responsibility." No lives were lost, but repairs cost some $20 million.

The French submarine *Siréne* also sank in dock at Lorient, an accident that was attributed to a faulty torpedo tube (October 11, 1972).

BATTERIES

The problem of a build-up of hydrogen gas while charging the batteries remained a major hazard in diesel-electric submarines, and the British A-class seems to have been particularly affected. HMS *Auriga* was running on the surface charging batteries during a NATO exercise off Gibraltar on February 12, 1970, when she was rocked by an explosion, but she made it back to port, carrying ten wounded. HMS *Alliance* suffered two battery explosions, the first also off Gibraltar in 1968 in which one man was injured. The second occurred in Portsmouth Naval Base on July 29, 1971, when a faulty air extraction system permitted the hydrogen level to build up and then a spark ignited it causing a major explosion. Again, nobody was seriously injured.

Far more serious than these two was the accident that occurred to HMS *Affray* in May 1951. She sailed from Portsmouth with a full crew of sixty-four, plus a further eleven, a mix of officers under training and Royal Marine Commandos. She disappeared without trace and her loss

Above: HMS *Affray* sailed from Portsmouth, England, in May 1951, with a crew of 64 and 11 passengers—and disappeared. The wreck was found some weeks later and the cause was attributed to either a broken snorkel tube or a battery gas explosion, or a combination of the two.

Left: HMS *Amphion*, a wartime submarine that was given a major modernization in the late 1950s. The A-class proved susceptible to a build-up of hydrogen during battery charging and there were several explosions, both in harbor and at sea.

Above: The fractured snorkel tube from HMS *Affray*, which was found on the seabed and recovered for detailed examination ashore. It is quite clear that the material had failed.

Below: The British spent many years experimenting with hydrogen peroxide as a fuel for both submarines and torpedoes. HMS *Sidon* was testing the torpedoes in 1955 when the notoriously volatile substance exploded, wrecking the inside of the submarine, causing eleven deaths, and sinking it. It was quickly raised, as seen here. The Russians failed to heed the lesson, resulting in the *Kursk* tragedy in 2000.

was a complete mystery until the wreck was found on June 14, 1951, lying at a depth of some 280 feet in the English Channel, some thirty miles north of the island of Guernsey. Underwater TV cameras discovered that the snorkel mast had split off a few feet above the deck pivot. This was not, however, considered to have been the sole cause of the tragedy and it was concluded that a gas explosion was almost certainly the main cause.

Another victim of battery gas explosion was the U.S. Navy's *Cochino*—see box.

HYDROGEN PEROXIDE

For many years designers searched for a method of powering a submerged submarine that contained its own air supply, known today as air-independent propulsion (AIP), and thus avoid the need for regular trips to the surface to recharge the batteries. One such system was developed in the 1930s by the gifted German engineer, Professor Helmut Walter, whose revolutionary concept for submarine propulsion centered on the use of high-test hydrogen peroxide (H_2O_2), usually known as HTP. This was stored in plastic bags outside the submarine pressure

hull, where the normal pressure of seawater forced the fuel into the boat, where it served as the oxidant in a closed-cycle diesel operation. No Walter-system U-boat became operational during the war, but after the German surrender the U.S., British and Soviet navies all examined and tested HTP systems.

The U.S. Navy's sole use of HTP was in *X-1*, a very small submarine based on the British wartime X-craft, but with a Walter-type propulsion system. She suffered a major internal explosion in February 1958, but was rebuilt with diesel engines and then served until 1973.

Britain's Royal Navy took Walter and his design team to the UK, together with one of his boats, and undertook lengthy trials, which led to the construction of two HTP-powered submarines, HMS *Explorer* and *Excalibur.* The sailors' attitude to these two boats is summed up in their nicknames—*Exploder* and *Excrutiator*—and although there were no major catastrophes, there were no regrets whatsoever when the boats were scrapped.

Walter's ideas were also pursued in the Soviet Union, leading to the Project 617 boat (NATO = Whale) and one prototype boat, *S-99.* This submarine achieved a total of

Above: Shaken survivors and rescue crews aboard a Motor Fishing Vessel (MFV) peer into the waters at Portland Naval Base, southern England, hoping to find more survivors from the sunken HMS *Sidon*.

ninety-eight voyages, a creditable performance. However, the Walter system was inherently unsafe and the final incident came on May 19, 1959, when a blockage in pipes carrying the HTP led to a build-up of pressure and then to an explosion. Her crew brought her to the surface and survived, but *S-99* never went to sea again.

What happened to HMS *Sidon* was far more serious. *Sidon* was involved in a testing program for a new torpedo, code-named Fancy, which used high-test peroxide as a fuel. On June 6, 1955, she was lying alongside her depot ship in Portland Naval Base, southern England, and preparations were being made for that day's test launch when a devastating explosion caused severe internal damage and took many lives. The subsequent inquiry established that a "hot run" had taken place inside the tube, which had over-pressurized the tubing inside the torpedo, causing an

HTP leak. When the HTP came into contact with copper in the torpedo it immediately reacted to form oxygen and steam. This caused the torpedo (not the warhead) to undergo a catastrophic disintegration, driving large segments of the torpedo and its tube down the length of the submarine with such force that even the watertight forward bulkhead was completely destroyed. The explosion killed twelve men of the crew, while the doctor of the depot ship, who had rushed aboard to treat the wounded, also perished when the submarine sank. As a result, the Royal Navy ceased using HTP, but the Soviet Navy was to use it many years later, with even more disastrous consequences, as described in the next chapter.

LIQUID OXYGEN

Another attempt at AIP was the Kreislauf closed-cycle system, which used liquid oxygen (LOX) to renew the oxygen content in the recycled exhaust gas. This was used operationally in the Soviet Malyutka-class (NATO = Quebec-class), launched in the 1950s. Unfortunately, LOX is a notoriously volatile substance, as witnessed by the ironic nickname given by Soviet sailors to the Malyutka-class—firelighters. According to Russian sources, five boats suffered major fires, but the only one recorded in the West is *M-256*, which, on September 26, 1957, suffered an explosion while submerged. The captain managed to bring her to the surface and ordered virtually all the crew onto the upper deck, while a few remained below to extinguish the blaze. After some four hours, the firefighters were forced to concede defeat and the captain ordered his crew to abandon ship, but the weather was so bad that only seven were rescued out of forty-two aboard.

NUCLEAR PROPULSION

This period saw the introduction of nuclear propulsion, with the first U.S. nuclear-propelled attack boat underway in January 1955, followed by a Russian one in July 1958, and a British boat in April 1963. In a world where the A-bomb attacks on Hiroshima and Nagasaki were very recent memories, the development of nuclear propulsion gave rise to very natural fears of disaster. These have never been realized, although there have been some very near scrapes, the Soviet Navy in particular having had a number of major problems.

One of the fundamental difficulties for the Soviet Navy was that it expanded very rapidly in the 1950s and '60s, leaping from a third-rate coastal force to the second largest fleet in the world with a global capability, and all within

some twenty years. Associated with this was a huge technological revolution, with the introduction of nuclear propulsion, a vast increase in the performance and capability of submarines, and the introduction of underwater-launched missiles.

Soviet overall designs were usually very sound and innovative, but detailed design was frequently poor and construction slipshod. These problems were exacerbated by routine maintenance being of a poor standard, although this was a widespread feature of life in the

former Soviet Union. The crews were also generally poorly trained and led by officers and warrant officers who had been promoted rapidly to meet the demands of the expanding navy. This lack of training was also not helped by the comparatively short time spent at sea compared to Western crews.

The first generation of Soviet nuclear submarines were of three types: Hotel-class—armed with strategic missiles (SSBN); Echo-class—cruise missiles (SSGN); and November-class—attack submarines (SSN). These were all powered with the same type of plant, which the West, not knowing its Soviet name, designated the "HEN" system, from the initial letters of the three types it powered.

The November-class suffered particularly badly. First-of-class *K-3* entered service in March 1959 and in June 1962

Below: Soviet November-class SSN, *K-3*, lies without power awaiting the arrival of rescue ships. This was not an unfamiliar sight in the Cold War, as the "HEN" nuclear-propulsion plant was dangerously unreliable, leading to many accidents and deaths.

incurred a steam generator fault, but, as far as is known, without casualties. Far more serious was a fire on September 8, 1967, in which thirty-nine men died; she returned to port but was taken out of service and her nuclear reactors were later dumped in the Kara Sea. *K-5* also had a severe reactor fault, but no further details are known.

K-8 returned to port in September 1961 with a crack in the steam generator plant, but in April 1970 she came to very public attention when she surfaced south of Land's End, England, with a serious fire aboard. She subsequently sank, taking fifty-two of her crew with her. *K-11* also had a severe reactor fault in February 1965 and was decommissioned, her reactor again being dumped in the Kara Sea.

Although outwardly very similar to other November-class boats, *K-27* differed in being powered by a liquid-metal reactor. She took a long time to build, but entered service in 1963 and then carried out two normal patrols. On her third patrol, however, there was a major problem in the steam-generator plant and in the thermal shielding, which resulted in nine deaths. She returned to port and was decommissioned, her hulk being scuttled in the White Sea on August 24, 1968.

An Echo II suffered a propulsion failure off the Kola peninsula in 1968, as a result of which she sank, taking ninety men to their deaths. This was almost certainly due to a problem in her reactor system.

PROJECT JENNIFER

Following a serious fire, *K-129*, a Soviet Golf II diesel-electric ballistic missile submarine, sank with the loss of all eighty-six crew in the central Pacific on April 11, 1968. The U.S. Navy knew the precise location of the wreck through its underwater sensor system, and the CIA funded and controlled an extraordinary operation to recover the boat, using the eccentric billionaire, Howard Hughes, as the public "front" for the operation. Code-named Operation Jennifer, a huge ship, the *Glomar Explorer*, was built and equipped specifically for this one operation. According to later reports she recovered the bow section, two nuclear-tipped torpedoes and a number of bodies, which were then given formal funerals. How true this was has never been established and the U.S. government remains tight-lipped on the subject to this day.

RAN AGROUND

Submarines occasionally ran aground. One such was USS *Tiru* (SS-416), a Guppy III, which had been exercising with Australian fleet units and was on passage from Brisbane to Subic Bay in the Philippines when she ran aground on the

Below: When a Soviet Golf II sank in the Pacific in 1968 the CIA mounted a complicated and expensive operation to recover its missiles and other equipment of intelligence interest.

Above: Post-war Guppies were converted World War Two U.S. Navy Gato- and Balao-class boats, streamlined and with greater battery capacity. Some remained in service for over 50 years; this is the Greek *Katsonis*, a Guppy III. They proved very reliable and had few accidents due to design faults.

Frederick Reef on November 3, 1963. With the boat having failed to get off under her own power, a tug and an Australian destroyer arrived which towed her off and she returned to Brisbane for emergency repairs. There were no casualties and, following repairs, she continued in service.

MISCELLANEOUS INCIDENTS

There were a number of other disasters during the period. The West German submarine *Hai* was originally built as *U-2365*, a Type XXIII, which was commissioned in March 1945 and sunk on May 8 that year. Together with ex-*U-2367*, it was raised in 1956, completely rebuilt and then returned to service. In September 1966 *Hai* was sailing across the North Sea on the surface en route to a visit to Aberdeen, Scotland, when it was overwhelmed by a wave, flooded, and sank; nineteen men died, and just one was saved.

China is very secretive about its navy in general and its submarines in particular, but one submarine is known to have been lost in December 1959. This was reputedly numbered *418* and thirty-nine men were killed, although a small number were reported to have escaped by the torpedo tubes.

NEAR MISSES

As in other periods, the margin between disaster and survival was sometimes very narrow. The officers of USS *Sargo* (SSN-583) took original action when their submarine caught fire in Pearl Harbor on June 14, 1960. Liquid oxygen was being pumped aboard when the inboard part of the line developed a leak, which, in turn, led to an explosion and fire in the stern torpedo room. Dockside firefighters were unable to bring the fire under control

quickly, so the senior officer present (the commanding officer was ashore) ordered that the after end be deliberately submerged with the torpedo hatch left open. This quickly extinguished the fire, although the damage from the fire and flooding took three months and several million dollars to repair. One man died trying to extinguish the blaze, but it could have been much worse.

There were also some quite unexpected dangers. An unnamed NATO submarine (probably either U.S. or British) was patrolling in the Barents Sea in October 1961 when the Soviets exploded a nuclear device, thought to be about 20MT. The explosion took place some 100 miles from the submarine, but caused considerable shock and some damage, although nobody was injured. The submarine surfaced to recover.

Overleaf: The *Glomar Explorer* was a huge, highly sophisticated and very expensive ship, built for one purpose only—the recovery of the sunken Soviet Golf II and the missiles it was carrying. It was not entirely successful, but showed American determination and use of high technology.

USS COCHINO (SS-345)

CLASS: Guppy II conversion.

DISPLACEMENT: submerged 2,420 tons.

DIMENSIONS: length 307 feet, beam 27 feet 4 inches.

PROPULSION: diesel-electric.

PERFORMANCE: surface 18 knots, submerged 16 knots; diving depth 400 feet.

ARMAMENT: 10 x 21-inch torpedo tubes (20 torpedoes).

CREW: 80.

U.S. Navy submarines *Cochino* (SS-345) and *Tusk* (SS-426) were snorkeling in a heavy Atlantic storm on August 26,

1949, when the constant operation of *Cochino*'s snorkel head valve led to a buildup of hydrogen, resulting in an explosion and fire in the after battery. The skipper ordered the battery room abandoned and brought the boat to the surface, with eighteen men in the engine room, aft of the isolated compartment.

Fire and fumes forced the forward crew topside, where lack of room on the bridge meant many had to stay on the open deck, lashed to the sail; one man was swept overboard but was rescued. Following more explosions below, the executive officer tried to disconnect the battery but was

severely burned. Then the diesels raced until their fuel was cut off by two engineers, following which the engine room was abandoned.

Tusk closed to transfer medical supplies and the dinghy was used to take two men on the return; both were swept into the sea but were rescued. At this point there were fourteen men on *Tusk*'s deck, but ten were swept overboard by a giant wave. Only three of these were rescued.

Aboard *Cochino* power was restored briefly, but the fire reasserted itself and "abandon ship" was ordered. In a daring operation *Tusk* rescued all *Cochino*'s survivors, the captain being the last to leave. Just one man was lost from *Cochino*, six from *Tusk*, all of whom had been swept off *Tusk*'s upper deck by the giant wave.

Below: USS *Cochino* (SS-345) was snorkeling in rough seas when a spark from an electrical device ignited a build-up of hydrogen. There was a major explosion and a fire, which eventually forced the crew to abandon ship. The captain, in accordance with the tradition of the sea, was the last to leave.

HMS TRUCULENT

CLASS: T-class.

DISPLACEMENT: submerged 1,571 tons.

DIMENSIONS: length 273 feet, beam 27 feet.

PROPULSION: diesel-electric.

PERFORMANCE: surface 15 knots, submerged 9 knots; diving depth 300 feet.

ARMAMENT: 11 x 21-inch torpedo tubes (17 torpedoes), 1 x 4-inch gun.

CREW: 63.

On January 12, 1950, the British submarine *Truculent* was returning to Sheerness, in south-east England, following post-refit trials, with eighteen dockyard workers aboard in addition to her crew. It was a cold and dark night and she was hit by Swedish tanker SS *Divina*; six men inside the submarine were killed and the five on the bridge were thrown into the water. They were picked up forty-five minutes later by a Danish ship.

The submarine sank, bottoming at 60 feet, where the sixty-seven survivors assembled to decide what to do. Hearing propellers overhead, they assumed that they were from rescue ships. There were insufficient Deep Submergence Emergency Apparatus (DSEA) sets, but this was

Above: The sinking of British submarine HMS *Truculent*, January 12, 1950, was yet another example of the difficulty of other ships, especially merchantmen, seeing a submarine in a crowded waterway at night.

resolved by giving non-swimmers priority. Once all was sorted out they began an orderly evacuation through the twill trunks in the control room and engine room. All went relatively smoothly in both places and most, if not all the men, reached the surface. But tragedy then struck. The men had no immersion suits, the propeller noises had been from normal traffic not rescue ships, the night was dark and the tide was strong. As a result, the men were scattered over a wide area and only ten were found alive; the remaining fifty met cold, lonely deaths.

Above: A group of survivors from *Truculent*. Although most of the 60-man crew escaped from the submarine and reached the surface, they were then scattered in the darkness and, lacking survival suits, met lonely deaths, only ten surviving.

Right: Swedish steamer *Divina*, showing the damage to her bows from hitting HMS *Truculent*.

USS THRESHER (SSN-593)

CLASS: Thresher.

DISPLACEMENT: submerged 4,311 tons.

DIMENSIONS: length 279 feet, beam 32 feet.

PROPULSION: nuclear.

PERFORMANCE: submerged 27 knots; diving depth 1,300 feet.

ARMAMENT: 4 x 21-inch torpedo tubes (24 torpedoes).

CREW: 94.

First of her class USS *Thresher* (SSN-593) suffered a series of problems during her first year of service with the U.S. Navy and was returned to the dockyard for work which was completed in March 1963. After several post-refit tests she sailed on April 10 for deep diving trials, accompanied by the rescue ship *Skylark*. Aboard were 112 naval men and 17 civilian observers.

Thresher dived on schedule at 0745 and made regular contact with *Skylark* until 0916, when a garbled message indicated that something was amiss, followed by breaking up noises, then silence. The full "Subsunk" procedure was implemented and a massive search was mounted. Some parts were dredged up, but eventually the bathyscaph *Trieste* photographed six separate sections on the seabed, which, together with debris, proved that *Thresher* had broken up and was lying at a depth of 8,400 feet.

Repeated and very detailed investigations have never conclusively established what happened, although the suspicions centered on welds on certain sections of piping. *Thresher* was the first nuclear-powered submarine to be lost, but no nuclear radiation has ever been detected from the site.

Below: *Thresher* seemed to epitomize everything that was excellent about American design and engineering, and her unexplained loss caused great public concern.

Below: *Thresher* (SSN-593) at sea. It was the first nuclear submarine to be lost. The reason remains a mystery to this day, although there has long been suspicion that the piping may have been involved.

USS SCORPION (SSN-589)

CLASS: Skipjack.

DISPLACEMENT: submerged 3,500 tons.

DIMENSIONS: length 252 feet, beam 32 feet.

PROPULSION: nuclear.

PERFORMANCE: submerged 30 knots; diving depth 700 feet.

ARMAMENT: 6 x 21-inch torpedo tubes (24 torpedoes).

CREW: 85.

USS *Scorpion* (SS-589) belonged to an earlier class than *Thresher*, but, like her, disappeared without explanation. She had been in the Mediterranean and was returning to her base at Norfolk, Virginia. At about 0800 on May 21, 1968, she sent a routine signal to her base reporting that she was some 250 miles west of the Azores, but after that—silence.

After a very lengthy search the wreck was found five months later in a position 450 miles south-west of the Azores, lying in one piece at a depth of some 11,000 feet. This was a considerable distance from her last reported position, something that has never been adequately explained. A report issued in 1993 stated that the reason for her loss was that a torpedo motor had started running and the captain decided to launch it to get rid of it. Unfortunately, according to this theory, it was a homing torpedo and once launched it circled, acquired *Scorpion* and homed on its launch vessel. It is true that several submarines have been sunk by their own torpedoes, but in this case, if true, it seems an incredible oversight by *Scorpion's* captain.

Above: USS *Scorpion* (SSN-589) was the second U.S. nuclear submarine to be lost and, as with *Thresher*, the cause has never been properly established.

Below: One suggested cause for *Scorpion's* loss is that a torpedo motor started to run and the captain ordered it to be launched, forgetting that it was a homer, and that there was no other target in the vicinity, but this seems improbable.

Right: When found, *Scorpion* was lying at a depth of 11,000 feet and some distance from her intended track, a discrepancy that remains a mystery. No other nuclear submarines have been lost by the U.S. Navy.

PART V: 1975-2005

Left: The period from the mid-1970s to the early 1990s marked the height of the Cold War, and the submarine fleets were in the front line. The scope for misunderstanding and accidents was great, but generally both sides played the game strictly according to the rules. One who did not was the captain of this Soviet Echo II-class submarine who had been followed by NATO anti-submarine forces throughout his voyage in the Mediterranean and eventually appears to have lost his temper and charged at one of his tormentors, a U.S. Navy frigate, USS *Voge* (DE-1047)—both vessels survived but were severely damaged.

PART V: 1975-2005

The period 1975 to 1992 saw the Cold War reach its greatest intensity, with many new nuclear-powered submarines, both missile-carrying and attack types, entering service, as well as increasing numbers of new-generation diesel-electric boats. The end of the Cold War then saw some reduction in naval activity and the once-proud Soviet Navy became a shadow of its former self, although many submarines continue to operate, and, as was dramatically shown by the Russian *Kursk* disaster, the potential for underwater tragedy is ever present.

One major change from earlier periods was that, while collisions between surface ships and submarines continued to occur, submarine hulls, particularly those of nuclear submarines, not only became much larger, in order to carry increasing numbers of weapons, but also much stronger, in order to operate at much greater depths. As a result, when submarines hit surface ships, it was now the latter that became the victim and suffered the worst losses, rather than vice versa.

FISHING BOATS

Although not major disasters in the sense of causing large numbers of casualties, there were many instances where submarines snagged fishing boat nets. With their immensely strong pressure hulls and powerful propulsion systems, the submarines almost invariably came off best, with minor damage and no casualties, but the fishermen underwent a very frightening and sometimes fatal experience. The fishing boats also lost their nets, which represented a substantial capital loss for the crews concerned, and one that was often not recovered, particularly from the Soviet Navy.

Below: German Type 209 submarines have a remarkable safety record; many have been in service for some thirty years, but none has ever been involved in a major disaster, although one did become entangled in North Sea fishing nets in 1984. This is *Nanggala* of the Indonesian Navy.

There were well over fifty recorded instances between 1976 and 1990, and many more that never reached the public domain. In most incidents the submarine snagged the nets and then dragged the fishing boat some distance while it tried to free itself without surfacing and thus enabling the fishermen to identify it. If forced to surface, the submarine's crew usually tried to free the nets manually, but if this failed, they had to resort to blow-torches or axes. The most serious outcome for the submarine was when the nets became entangled with the propeller and thus were beyond the crew's capability to free them, in which case the submarine had to be towed to the nearest suitable port.

A typical incident took place on August 8, 1984, in the English Channel, where the British trawler *Joanne C* suddenly found itself being towed by an underwater object—clearly a submarine—that had become enmeshed in its nets. This continued for some three hours, during which the crew contacted the U.S. Coast Guard for help, to be told that, while there were no American submarines in the area, the Royal Navy admitted that one of theirs was, but claimed that it was some thirty miles away. Believing from this that the submarine involved must be a Soviet one, the fishermen cut their lines and the nets were lost. The Royal Navy, however, had a policy of paying compensation when the fault was demonstrably theirs, and when some weeks later the boat's owner received a check for some £2,000 (about $1,050) it was a tacit confirmation of responsibility.

A much more serious incident, also in European waters, took place on March 29, 1984, when a West German-built Type 209 diesel-electric submarine, on builder's trials in the North Sea prior to delivery to the Chilean Navy, became entangled in the nets of the small Danish fishing boat *Ane Katherin*. The boat was dragged under, killing all three crew.

It was unusual for the submarine to come off worst, but that happened to a North Korean Yugo-class boat during a spying mission in 1998. The Communist state built some forty of these boats, which displaced 98 tons, carried a crew of two and seven special forces operators, and were specifically designed for espionage missions against South Korea. On

Above: Another, and much more sinister, incident took place in 1998, when a North Korean Yugo-class submarine on a spying mission became inextricably entangled in South Korean fishing nets. When the submarine was eventually opened it was found that all the crew were dead.

June 22 this particular boat became inextricably entangled in South Korean fishermen's nets and had to be freed by the South Korean Navy. The latter then started towing it to the nearest port, but it sank, possibly due to the action of the crew who were still enclosed inside. When the South Koreans eventually managed to gain access they discovered that all the

INCIDENTS INVOLVING SUBMARINES AND FISHING BOATS: 1976-2005		
COUNTRY	**SUBMARINE**	**FISHING BOATS**
DENMARK	2	4
FRANCE	2	5
GERMANY	3	2
IRELAND		6
JAPAN	1	4
NORTH KOREA	1	0
NORWAY		6
SOUTH KOREA		1
SPAIN		3
UK	17	13
US	13	5
USSR/RUSSIA	11	1
UNKNOWN	4	4
TOTALS	54	54

crew were dead—five had been shot in the body, four in the head—so who killed whom was never clear.

The locations of these submarine involvements with fishing boats were spread around the world's oceans and seas: Atlantic—14; Baltic—2; Barents Sea—3; English Channel—4; Irish Sea—13; Sea of Japan—3; Mediterranean—1; North Sea—6; Norwegian Sea—1; and Pacific—7. In the course of these events, thirty-seven fishermen were drowned (thirty of them in the Japanese disaster), while a further nine were murdered or committed suicide in the North Korean submarine. In material terms, four fishing boats were sunk, two suffered major damage and thirteen minor damage, while thirty-two lost their nets, although many navies

radar, and when under sail were virtually silent and thus undetectable by sonar. Despite this, recorded collisions were relatively few, just four in the 1980s, for example, in which two yachts were sunk and two damaged, but without loss of life.

NAVIGATION ERRORS

Navigational errors by submarines fell into two categories—hitting the seabed through miscalculation, and running aground while proceeding on the surface—and there were several examples of each. The most spectacular example took place on October 27, 1981, when Soviet *S-137*, a Whiskey-class diesel-electric submarine, ran aground some six miles from the main Swedish naval base at Karlskrona, demonstrating beyond doubt to the world's media that it had violated the territorial waters of a neutral nation. The captain maintained that his error was due to a combination of bad weather and a faulty compass, which the Swedish government refused to accept. The Soviets did little to help their case when they sent a tug and a submarine to try to tow *S-137* off, but their unauthorized entry into Swedish territorial waters resulted in them being turned back by the Swedish Navy. The Swedes also announced that there was evidence of nuclear weapons aboard (presumably torpedoes) but having thoroughly humiliated the Soviets they allowed the submarine to leave on November 6.

COLLISIONS—NAVAL

The increasing intensity of the Cold War resulted in collisions between Soviet and NATO—particularly U.S.—warships and submarines. In August 1976, NATO detection systems picked up Soviet submarine *K-22* (Echo II-class) passing through the Straits of Gibraltar, and U.S. Navy aircraft and submarines then shadowed the boat closely until, on August 28, it surfaced near the frigate USS *Voge* (FF-1047). After running past at speed, it turned in and deliberately rammed the American ship in the port quarter. There were no casualties among either crew, but both vessels were seriously damaged, although they made it back to their respective bases. The collision took place in

stated unofficially that they thought that some of these claims were exaggerated, and on some occasions, totally made-up.

YACHTS

Yachts were a different matter, since they were made of wood or fiberglass, which made them difficult to see on

Above: A 1976 collision in the Mediterranean took place after a Soviet submarine had been tracked for many days by U.S. anti-submarine forces, including aircraft and surface ships, such as the Bronstein-class destroyer escort, USS *McCloy* (DE-1038).

Right: Having charged straight at USS *Voge* at high speed, the Soviet Echo II-class took last minute evasive action, as seen here, either because the submarine captain was overpowered by his crew or because he had last-second doubts about the stupidity of what he was doing.

broad daylight and the Soviet captain was clearly aware of *Voge's* presence; indeed, photographs taken from the U.S. ship show the submarine making straight towards it. The general belief was that the captain was either frustrated at his inability to shake off his relentless shadowers, or drunk (or both), lost his temper and decided to teach the Americans a lesson.

On February 11, 1992, *Barrakuda*, a Sierra I-class attack submarine, was on the surface off Kildin Island near Severodvinsk when it carried out a routine submergence. Unknown to *Barrakuda*, it was being shadowed by U.S. submarine *Baton Rouge* (SSN-689). When the Soviet submarine dived it was so close that the U.S. boat temporarily lost track of it and the two boats hit each other. Both managed to return to their bases, but were so severely damaged that neither was repairable and never

Right: Two Soviet submarines pass each other off the Kola Inlet, one inbound, the other setting out on patrol. Considering the number of submarines at sea during the Cold War, it is astonishing that there were so few incidents.

Above: USS *George Washington* (SSBN-598) was the U.S. Navy's first-ever nuclear-powered strategic missile submarine, carrying sixteen Polaris missiles in two rows of eight vertically mounted silos abaft the sail.

Left: The damage to USS *George Washington*'s sail after the collision with the Japanese freighter *Nissho Maru*, 2,350 tons. The impact sank the freighter, the reverse of pre-World War Two collisions, where it was almost invariably the submarine that sank.

Right: Soviet Victor-class attack submarines were involved in several incidents, including a 1984 collision in the Straits of Gibraltar when one was trying to avoid NATO detection by hiding under a Soviet tanker. A sudden upsurge drove the submarine into the tanker's bottom, causing considerable damage, leaving the submarine captain with no option but to surface.

returned to service. The collision gave rise to heated diplomatic exchanges, full details of which have never been made public.

A different type of collision took place during a major naval exercise in the Caribbean on October 31, 1983. Frigate USS *McCloy* (FF-1038) was towing a linear sonar array when the cable suddenly went slack. On hauling it in it was discovered that a large part of the array had disappeared. The following day a Soviet Victor III SSN was discovered lying stationary on the surface by a U.S. Navy P-3 patrol aircraft. It was apparently unable to proceed, although it appeared undamaged. It was eventually towed to Cuba by a Soviet merchant ship. It is believed that the Victor III was tracking *McCloy* and got so close to the sonar array (without, it would appear, being

detected) that the latter, a substantial device some four inches in diameter, fouled the submarine's propellers, breaking off at least one of the blades.

COLLISIONS—SUBMARINE/CIVILIAN

On April 9, 1981, in the South China Sea some thirty miles off the Japanese coast, nuclear-powered ballistic missile submarine USS *George Washington* (SSBN-598) was running at periscope depth when it collided with the Japanese-registered 2,350-ton freighter, *Nissho Maru*. The submarine suffered only minor damage to its sail, but the smaller Japanese ship sank within fifteen minutes, taking two men to their deaths. There were thirteen survivors, but the submarine failed to see them and left the scene, a problem made worse when the U.S. Navy failed to tell the

Japanese authorities until some eighteen hours later, and the survivors were not rescued until some twenty hours after that. The U.S. Navy admitted liability, paid some $3 million compensation, and relieved the commanding officer, thus virtually ending his naval career.

In another incident, the Japanese submarine *Nadashio*, was traveling on the surface in Tokyo Bay on July 23, 1988, when it found itself facing two oncoming civilian boats on converging courses. The submarine reduced speed, thus avoiding one boat, but making a collision with the other inevitable. The victim was the sport fishing boat, *No. 1 Fuji Maru*, which sank within two minutes, with twenty-eight dead and nineteen rescued, of whom all but two were injured. Both vessels were found to be partially at fault and their captains were sentenced to terms of imprisonment—the captain of *Nadashio* for two years and that of *Fuji Maru* to one, although both sentences were

later reduced to four years' probation. The Japanese government paid $17 million in compensation and the head of the Japanese Maritime Self Defense Force (JMSDF) resigned.

On August 26, 1988, the Peruvian submarine *Pacocha* (formerly USS *Atule*) was on the surface off the coast of Peru in the Pacific Ocean, returning from a torpedo exercise, when at 1850 local time it was rammed aft by a Japanese trawler. Unfortunately, the Japanese vessel was fitted with a strengthened bow for Antarctic operations, and *Pacocha* sank within minutes, settling on the bottom at about 140 feet at an upward angle of about twelve degrees. There were forty-nine aboard; twenty-three escaped as the submarine sank, but twenty-six went down with the boat, of whom twenty-two were still alive. The trawler's crew did not realize what they had hit, while the submarine sank before any radio message could be transmitted, leading to a delay in activating rescue

procedures. The alarm was not raised ashore until about an hour later. As a result, rescue ships only arrived in the area some two-and-a-half hours after the sinking, where their first task was to pick up twenty men in the water; sadly, due to the delay, the other three had already died of exposure.

The surviving men in the submarine acted very calmly and sensibly, retreated into the forward compartment, took every precaution to avoid polluting the atmosphere, and released emergency buoys and flares. At Peruvian request, the U.S. Navy activated its emergency McCann rescue team, which started the flight to Peru. But they turned back on being informed that, as pollution was increasing, the survivors had been ordered to make individual escapes.

The men inside the submarine escaped in batches of four, using the U.S. Navy Steinke hood method, the last leaving some twenty-three hours after the collision. Unfortunately, there were delays in processing so many

men through the one available decompression chamber, so that one man died, one was severely brain-damaged, and several others developed decompression sickness. The survivors behaved excellently and it was very sad that the facilities on the surface were unable to cope.

There were several collisions between ships and submarines of the Soviet Navy, one of which, on September 18, 1984, involved a Victor I SSN making a clandestine transit of the Straits of Gibraltar by hiding inside the "noise shadow" underneath a Soviet tanker. The Straits are, however, notorious for their unexpected thermal gradients and one of these thrust the Victor I upwards so that it hit the bottom of the tanker. The outer casing of the submarine's bows was totally ripped off, allowing fascinated NATO observers an unusual glimpse of its sonar array and torpedo tubes. The submarine limped to the Soviet Navy's anchorage on the Tunisian coast and then returned to Severomorsk in October.

On October 24, 1981, *S-178*, an elderly Whiskey-class diesel-electric boat, was hit by an unidentified refrigerator ship off Vladivostok and sank with all hands. This was a major tragedy, but took place in Soviet-controlled waters, which were closed to Western media. In any case, it was quickly pushed out of the headlines when *S-137*, also a Whiskey-class boat, ran aground off Sweden, under circumstances much more accessible to the press (see above).

CAUSE UNKNOWN

During the period, as usual, a number of submarines disappeared due to unknown causes—or, if the reasons were known to the authorities, they were not released. The first was the Pakistani mini-submarine, *SX-404*, which disappeared off Karachi on January 2, 1977, taking eight men to their deaths. Second was yet another Soviet Echo-class, *K-429*, which sank on June 24, 1983, off Kamchatka. It was later salvaged, during which it was discovered that all the crew rations had been consumed, indicating that some, at least, of the crew had suffered dreadful deaths on the seabed. Finally, two Romeo-class diesel-electric boats disappeared—one Chinese, in 1987, the other North Korean, on February 20, 1988. The North

Left: At least two Chinese-built Romeo-class submarines have suffered disasters. A Chinese-manned Romeo sank in 1987 and there have been persistent rumors that some of the crew escaped through the torpedo tubes. The other, a North Korean boat, sank with all hands in 1988.

Above: This damaged Echo II-class boat was limping home to a Soviet port when it was photographed by a British Nimrod aircraft. The large wells in the casing channeled the efflux from the cruise-missile engines and caused great underwater turbulence, making these boats easy to track.

Korean boat went down with all hands, but unconfirmed rumors suggest that in the latter case some of the crew escaped through the torpedo tubes.

SOVIET NAVY NUCLEAR ACCIDENTS

Despite sophisticated modern technology, coupled with advanced system monitoring and warning devices, submarines continued to be disabled by nuclear-related events, particularly in the Soviet fleet. Of these incidents, the majority involved the Echo-class, powered by the notorious HEN nuclear propulsion system, most of

which followed a similar pattern. In this, the submarine surfaced emitting smoke, and most of the crew then assembled on the open deck dressed in nuclear protection gear, leaving the bare minimum of crewmen below to fight the fire. The boat then lay stationary, because the

SOVIET NAVY NUCLEAR-RELATED INCIDENTS: 1976-2005					
DATE	SUBMARINE	CLASS	PLACE	DEAD	REMARKS
Sep 26, 1976	K-47	Echo II	Atlantic	8	Fire
1977	Unknown	Echo II	Indian Ocean	n/k	Towed to Vladivostok
Aug 19, 1978	K-116	Echo II	Atlantic	n/k	Nuclear problem; towed home
1979	K-45	Echo I	n/k	n/k	Towed home
Aug 21, 1980	K-122	Echo I	Philippine Sea	9+	Towed to Vladivostok
Aug 8, 1982	K-123	Alfa	Barents Sea		Coolant leak
Jun 24, 1983	K-429	Charlie I	North Pacific	100	Sunk; salvaged Aug 1983
Aug 21, 1983	K-122	Echo I	Off Okinawa	9	Underwater fire
Nov 2, 1983	Victor III	Victor III	Caribbean	n/k	Fire; towed to Cuba
Jun 18, 1984	K-131	Echo II	Barents Sea	13	Fire
Oct 6, 1986	K-219	Yankee	East of Bermuda	4+	Internal explosion; sank
Apr 7, 1989	K-278	Mike	Off Norwegian coast	42	Electrical fire; explosion
Jun 25, 1989	K-192	Echo II	Norwegian Sea	n/k	Radiation accident
Sep 27, 1991	Typhoon	Typhoon	Arctic	n/k	Missile launch malfunction

automated safety systems had taken the nuclear reactor off-line, although the control rods still had to be lowered manually, often at great risk to the sailors concerned. Eventually, water began to enter the hull, which then lost stability and sank. In each known case, the nuclear shutdown machinery functioned successfully, although the boat had to be towed back to port, where it was then usually taken out of service.

Several Echo IIs that suffered reactor problems remain hulked in Russian ports. *K-431* has been at Pavlovsk, near Vladivostok, since December 1985, and *K-192* at Polyarny since June 1989. Indeed, it was the official investigation into the latter accident that revealed a number of basic design faults, leading to all surviving submarines powered by the HEN propulsion system being withdrawn from service.

There have also been problems with missiles. The Yankee I-class SSBNs carried sixteen SS-N-6 strategic

Below: Yankee I SSBN *K-219* was forced to surface in the Caribbean when a missile warhead caught fire, generating choking smoke throughout the boat. One problem led to another and the captain eventually had to scuttle her, and she now lies on the Atlantic seabed.

missiles, and *K-219* of this class suffered two accidents with its missiles while inside their tubes. The first was on August 31, 1973, but this seems to have been fairly minor; the second, in October 1986, was much more serious. The submarine was cruising on station near Bermuda when an explosion in one of the missile tubes resulted in the missile compartment filling with smoke, steam and fumes, and the captain immediately brought his boat to the surface. Fire raged in the missile compartment and water began to enter the hull, leading to an electrical problem that activated the nuclear shutdown procedures, and a sailor then died while struggling to lower the fuel rods. At this stage water started to enter the main ballast tank and the boat steadily lost buoyancy. One of the faithful Soviet merchant ships then arrived and most of the submarine crew were transferred, leaving the captain and eight others. But after a few more hours, these, too, had to abandon the submarine, which sank at 1103 on October 6, with the loss of four more lives. Various theories have been advanced regarding the start of the fire, including that the submarine was hit by a U.S. Navy SSN, but none has ever been proven.

Below: In 1991 a Soviet Typhoon-class SSBN launched a missile whose motor failed to work properly and it fell back onto the upper deck. This caused some damage but the giant boat was very strong and returned safely to port.

Another missile accident occurred when a giant Typhoon-class SSBN conducted a live missile launch in the Arctic in September 1991. The vessel was apparently on the surface and launching a series of missiles in succession when one of them suffered a motor malfunction and fell back onto the submarine, which then ended the exercise and returned safely to port.

The Alfa-class were very high performance attack boats, powered by two liquid-metal (lead-bismuth) reactors and using a revolutionary titanium hull. The prototype suffered a freeze-up of its metal coolant and had to be scrapped, but second-of-class *K-123* was more successful until August 8, 1982, when there was a leak in the steam generator, which led to a large quantity of metal coolant leaking into the reactor compartment and solidifying. There were no known deaths and the submarine returned to port, but the Soviet Navy then devoted no less than nine years to rebuilding her, but this time with a pressurized-water reactor.

THE *KURSK* TRAGEDY

Undoubtedly the greatest tragedy during this period was the loss of the Russian nuclear-powered, missile-carrying submarine, Oscar II-class *Kursk*. The Russian Navy's Northern Fleet held a major exercise in the Barents Sea in August 2000, with the fleet commander flying his flag in the battle cruiser *Pyotr Velikhiy* (Peter the Great). As part of

Above: Soviet Oscar-class cruise-missile launcher *Kursk* made headlines around the world when it sank in August 2000. An international effort was mounted to rescue the crew but without success, and the whole incident highlighted the poor state of the Russian Navy.

the exercise, the *Kursk* successfully launched several Granit (SS-N-19) missiles on August 10 and 11. The exercise then moved into its next phase on Saturday, August 12, which involved several submarines carrying out simulated torpedo attacks against the main group of surface warships.

At about 0728 GMT, sonars aboard *Pyotr Velikhiy* detected an underwater blast, followed two minutes later by a second and much more powerful explosion that actually rocked the huge battle cruiser. Those aboard *Pyotr Velikhiy* failed to see any significance and carried on with the exercise, and it was only about nine hours later that the absence of reports from *Kursk* began to cause concern. A search was then instigated, but it took some thirty hours to locate the submarine, which was lying inert on the seabed at a depth of some 350 feet.

From the start, the Russian handling of public relations was appalling and frequently contradictory, an early example being that on Monday, August 14, it was claimed that radio contact with the *Kursk* had been made, only for this to be denied shortly afterwards, with the admission that the only means of contact was by knocking on the hull. Similarly, spokesmen tried to blame the loss on collision with a foreign submarine, which was vehemently denied by the British and U.S. governments, although both admitted that they had submarines in the general

area: USS *Memphis* (SSN-691) and *Toledo* (SSN-769), and HMS *Splendid*, respectively. Since the exercise took place in international waters, these submarines had every right to be there and it was perfectly normal for U.S. and British warships to monitor Russian exercises, and vice versa.

Russian rescue attempts were hampered by three factors: appalling surface weather, strong currents, and the angle at which *Kursk* was lying.

Thus, even when a Russian submersible reached the submarine it was unable to latch on due to the angle. Two further issues became politically very sensitive. The first was that Russian President Putin was on holiday and for some days refused to return to Moscow to take personal charge, the second that the Russian authorities would not accept foreign offers of help until late on August 16, when Norwegian and British offers were accepted. By now it was generally accepted that there was little prospect of any survivors remaining alive, but desperate rescue efforts continued. The British LR5 submersible reached the area aboard a chartered ship, but was not deployed, although Norwegian divers reached the submarine on August 20 and the following day the same divers opened *Kursk*'s after hatch, but found the airlock below flooded. A few hours later they managed to open the airlock's inner hatch, only to find that the hull, too, was flooded, and the divers reluctantly confirmed that there was no prospect of life aboard.

American authorities stated early on that one of their monitoring submarines had detected two explosions in the area. This was later confirmed by the Norwegian seismological institute, Norsar, which stated that it had

Below: The British LR5 submersible was developed from a diver lock-out vehicle for the oil industry. It has proved extremely successful and is on constant call for submarine disasters anywhere in the world.

detected two powerful explosions in the Barents Sea area at about 0728 and 0730 GMT on August 12; the first was equivalent to about 100kg and the second to a massive 2 tonnes of TNT. These two explosions devastated the forward part of the submarine, instantly killing approximately two-thirds of the crew. The remaining men were aft and survived for some hours, before suffering a terrible death.

Canadian submarine HMCS *Chicoutimi* was bought from the British Royal Navy and completely refitted before being taken over and sailing for Halifax, Canada. On the

morning of October 5, 2004, she was heading westwards across the Atlantic, some 100 miles north-west of Ireland, and sailing on the surface in stormy weather. Urgent repair work on a valve in the upper tower hatch required both lids to be open, with the result that when a high wave broke over the tower a considerable amount of water cascaded down inside the submarine. This was quickly mopped up, but two hours later an electrical fire started and, although it was quickly controlled, acrid smoke spread through the boat causing a number of inhalation casualties. Then some six hours later oxygen generators were run to clear the air, but this caused another fire, which, again, was extinguished. Rescue vessels and helicopters were soon on the scene but one officer died. The Board of Enquiry reviewed all the events in detail and decided that nobody was to blame.

Below: HMCS *Chicoutimi* under tow (towing ship is off picture, left) with frigate HMS *Montrose* standing by and a Royal Navy Merlin helicopter hovering overhead. One man died and several were injured in the mid-Atlantic fire, which took place on the delivery voyage to Canada.

SOVIET K-278

CLASS: Mike.

DISPLACEMENT: submerged 8,500 tons.

DIMENSIONS: length 386 feet, beam 35 feet.

PROPULSION: nuclear.

PERFORMANCE: submerged 31 knots; diving depth 3,300 feet.

ARMAMENT: 6 x 21-inch torpedo tubes.

CREW: 57.

The sole titanium-hulled Mike-class SSN, *Komsomolets*, was cruising at a depth of 1,250 feet when, at 1101 on April 7, 1989, fire erupted in the steering compartment. The blaze spread to the next compartment but also generated a power surge through the boat's electrics, causing new fires elsewhere. The nuclear plant was automatically shut down and at about 1120 the captain surfaced and transmitted an SOS, while his crew fought the blaze.

The raging inferno melted some welds and the captain ordered abandon ship. Several life rafts were launched, but only one 25-man raft could be used, and some of the fifty men had to cling to the outside. Aircraft arrived overhead at 1440 and dropped more rafts. Six men were still in the submarine when it went down at 1708, of whom five scrambled into the escape capsule. The release mechanism jammed, but functioned when the submarine bottomed, and the capsule then shot to the surface. Of the men inside, one survived, two were blown into the water and never seen again, and the other two died from toxic fumes.

In all, twenty-nine men survived, two of whom died later. Of the forty-two lost, four had perished due to the fires and explosions, the remainder due to drowning or exposure.

Below: Soviet Mike-class attack submarine *Komsomolets* was the victim of a fire while submerged. There were forty-two deaths, four due to fires and thirty-eight to drowning or exposure after abandoning ship; twenty-nine survived.

USS GREENEVILLE (SSN-772)

CLASS: Los Angeles.

DISPLACEMENT: submerged 6,900 tons.

DIMENSIONS: length 360 feet, beam 33 feet.

PROPULSION: nuclear.

PERFORMANCE: submerged 31 knots; diving depth 1,480 feet.

ARMAMENT: 4 x 21-inch torpedo tubes.

CREW: 127.

Over the years there have been numerous collisions between submarines and surface ships, but none as curious—or as inexcusable—as that involving USS *Greeneville*. On February 9, 2001, the Los Angeles-class nuclear attack submarine was on a one-day training exercise from its Pearl Harbor base, carrying a party of sixteen civilian guests. These guests were looked after well and, following a lengthy lunch, the commanding officer decided to demonstrate an "emergency main ballast blow." The submarine shot to the surface, but,

unfortunately, directly beneath a Japanese civilian fishery training ship, *Ehime Maru*, whose presence had clearly not been detected. The Japanese ship was severely damaged, with nine aboard missing and presumed dead and twelve needing hospital treatment; there were no injuries aboard *Greeneville*.

Subsequent official investigations established that civilians were at some of the submarine's controls (albeit under close supervision), the sonar room chief was serving as a tour guide, there was a minor sonar malfunction, and the surfacing procedures were rushed because the tour program was behind schedule. As in so many accidents, it was a combination of these problems, none of them acute in itself, which led to the tragedy.

Below: USS *Greeneville* shows her damaged rudder as she returns to Pearl Harbor, February 10, 2001, following the accident with *Ehime Maru*. The accident took place nine miles south of Hawaii during a public relations cruise.

Below: Japanese ship *Ehime Maru* was hit from underneath by *Greeneville*, which was surfacing. This picture gives an indication of the force exerted by a large modern nuclear submarine, with its immensely strong pressure hull, especially when hitting the unprotected bottom of a somewhat smaller civilian ship.

SOVIET KURSK (K-141)

CLASS: Oscar II.

TYPE: nuclear-powered, cruise-missile carrier.

DISPLACEMENT: submerged 19,400 tons.

DIMENSIONS: length 505 feet, beam 60 feet.

PROPULSION: nuclear.

PERFORMANCE: submerged 31 knots; diving depth 2,000 feet.

ARMAMENT: 24 x SS-N-19 cruise missiles; 4 x 21-inch torpedo tubes; 4 x 26-inch torpedo tubes.

CREW: 107.

Above: The Russian Navy suffered from low morale after the collapse of the Soviet Union, but one source of great pride was the *Kursk*, which was often featured in publicity pictures, such as in this crew inspection.

Oscar-II class SSGNs are huge submarines, carrying twenty-four cruise-missiles, a concept unique to the Soviet/Russian Navy. The missile launchers are in bins mounted outside the hull, hence the 60-foot beam, while there are eight torpedo tubes in the bows, for which twenty-four weapons are carried, including SS-N-16 torpedoes.

The submarine *Kursk (K-141)* was taking part in fleet maneuvers in the Barents Sea on August 12, 2000, when it was racked by two catastrophic explosions, some two minutes apart. NATO was monitoring the exercise and news of the disaster quickly spread around the world, particularly because it was soon known that the submarine in trouble was both nuclear-powered and also armed with nuclear weapons. The Russians quickly located the hulk, which was lying at a depth of some 300 feet and at a considerable angle; there was heavy damage to the bow, but no sign of life among the 118 known to have been aboard.

Russian naval vessels quickly assembled in the area, but rescue operations were severely hampered by poor weather and sea conditions, while both Russian and international opinion became highly critical of the very obvious reluctance of the naval leaders to accept any of the many offers of outside help. Partly, this reluctance was because they wanted to look after their own problems, but they were also concerned that such rescuers might take advantage of the opportunity to see inside a modern Russian submarine. Divers managed to reach the submarine a week later and opened one of the hatches, but by that stage there was no hope of any survivors.

Some Russians immediately tried to blame external forces, one theory that was widely aired being that a British or U.S. submarine had trailed *Kursk* too closely and collided with her. NATO quickly admitted that there had been submarines in the general area, but this was common practice, and they gave public assurances that none had been anywhere near the Russian submarine at the time of the disaster.

It eventually came to light that the SS-N-15 was a new torpedo forced on the Russian Navy for economical reasons. Older torpedoes were battery-powered, which required expensive silver components, but the new weapons used a turbojet with hydrogen peroxide as the oxidizer. A highly corrosive substance, the hydrogen peroxide had probably escaped, causing the first explosion and generating a fire that led to the second. Once the process had started, *Kursk* and those aboard her never stood a chance.

Left: *Kursk* at sea. The explosion in the torpedo originated with the hydrogen peroxide oxidant, which had been introduced, despite its well-known dangers, as an economy measure.

SUBMARINE ACCIDENTS 1774-2005

This table lists all known accidental losses of submarines, excluding:

A) losses due to enemy action, but including wartime losses not due to enemy action;

B) losses in dockyards when in dockyard hands or when under tow;

but including:

A) losses where submarine sank but was later recovered;

B) significant accidents where the submarines did not sink, but there was loss of life or the submarine became non-operational.

Abbreviations: s/m = submarine; m/s = merchant ship; u/k = unknown; "Op loss; cause unknown" means that a submarine failed to return from a patrol (either in war or peace) and subsequent research has failed to establish a definite explanation.

DATE	SUBMARINE	COUNTRY	LOCATION	CAUSE	DIED
June 20, 1774	Maria	UK	Plymouth Sound	Not known	1
1831	Cervo	Spain	u/k	Bad design	1
1834	Petit	France	St Valery	Bad design	1
Feb 1, 1851	Brandtaucher	Germany	Kiel harbor	Human error	0
1851	Phillip	USA	Lake Erie	Dived too deep	1
1863	Hunley	Confed	Charleston harbor	Swamped	8
1863	Hunley	Confed	Charleston	Foundered in storm	6
1863	Hunley	Confed	Ft Johnson, Charleston	Capsized in collision	5
Oct 15, 1863	Hunley	Confed	Stone River, Charleston	Diving error	9
Feb 17, 1864	Hunley	Confed	Charleston Roads	Entangled with target	7
April 1865	Plongeur	France	Rochefort	Bad design	0
1866	Flach	Chile	Valparaiso Bay	Bad design	8
1868	Potpourri	Russia	St Petersburg	Bad design	1?
May 22, 1878	Holland II	USA	Upper Passaic River, NJ	Human error	0
1887	Nautilus	USA	Tilbury	Bad design	0
Mar 18, 1904	A.1	UK	Spithead	Collision; m/s SS Berwick Castle	11
June 29, 1904	Delfin	Russia	River Neva	Swamped by m/s	21
June 8, 1905	A.8	UK	Plymouth Sound	Gas explosion on surface	15
July 6, 1905	Farfadet	France	Lake Bizerta	Human error; hatch not secured	14
Oct 16, 1905	A.4	UK	Stokes Bay Portsmouth	Swamped; human error	0
1906	A.9	UK	Off Plymouth	Collision; m/s; saved by release of drop keel	0
Aug 13, 1906	Esturgeon	France	Saigon	Sank in dock	0
Oct 17, 1906	Lutin	France	Lake Bizerta	Leaks in hull; sank	14
Jan 17, 1907	Algerien	France	Cherbourg Dockyard	Human error	0
June 13, 1907	C.8	UK	Portsmouth	Petrol vapor explosion	3
June 19, 1907	Gymnote	France	Toulon	Human error; flooded in dock	2
April 26, 1909	Foca	Italy	Naples harbor	Internal explosion	14
June 12, 1909	Kambala	Russia	Off Sevastopol	Collision; battleship	23
July 14, 1909	C.11	UK	Off Cromer	Collision; m/s	13
July 14, 1909	C.16/C.17	UK	Off Cromer	Collided with each other	0
April 15, 1910	No 6	Japan	Off Kure, Hiroshima Bay	Ventilator valve flooded	14
May 26, 1910	Pluviose	France	Off Calais	Collision; ferry Pas de Calais	27
Nov 17, 1911	U-3	Germany	Kiel harbor	Human error; ventilator open	3
Feb 2, 1912	A.3	UK	Off Isle of Wight	Collision; HMS Hazard	14
June 8, 1912	Vendemaire	France	Off Cherbourg	Collision; battleship	24
Oct 4, 1912	B.2	UK	Off Dover	Collision; m/s	15
Oct 11, 1912	F.1 (SS-20)	USA	Port Watsonville, CA	Broke moorings in heavy sea	2
April 6, 1913	Minoga	Russia	Off Libau	Foundered on test dive	0
Dec 10, 1913	C.14	UK	Plymouth Sound	Collision with Hopper No 27	0
Jan 8, 1913	E.5	UK	Portsmouth	Engine room explosion	3
Jan 16, 1914	A.7	UK	Whitesand Bay	Diving failure; cause unknown	11
Jan 31, 1914	O-5	Neth	Scheldt Quay	Mechanical failure; tubes open	1
March 1914	Minoga	Russia	Off Libau	Vent open when diving	0

DATE	SUBMARINE	COUNTRY	LOCATION	CAUSE	DIED
July 7, 1914	Calypso	France	Off Cape Lardier	Collision; submarine Circe	3
Sep 14, 1914	AE-1	Australia	Bismarck Sea	Op loss; cause unknown	30
Jan 17, 1915	Saphir	France	Dardanelles	Ran aground	14
Jan 21, 1915	U-7	Germany	North Sea	Sunk in error by U-22	26
Mar 25, 1915	Skate (SS-23)	USA	Honolulu	Foundered; corrosion of battery tank caused flooding	21
May 1915	UB-3	Germany	Mediterranean	Op loss; cause unknown	14
Aug 18, 1915	E.13	UK	Saltholm Flat	Ran aground	15
Oct 30, 1915	Turquoise	France	Dardanelles	Ran aground	0
Nov 4, 1915	UC-8	Germany	Terschelling	Ran aground	0
Nov 19, 1915	UC-13	Germany	Black Sea	Foundered in storm	0
Dec 5, 1915	Fresnel	France	Albanian coast	Stranded in fog; human error	0
Jan 15, 1916	Sturgeon (SS-25)	USA	Brooklyn Navy Yard	Internal explosion	5
Jan 16, 1916	E.17	UK	Dutch coast, off Texel	Wrecked; bad weather	0
Jan 19, 1916	H.6	UK	Off Ameland Island	Ran aground	0
April 27, 1916	UC-5	Germany	Off Harwich	Ran aground	0
May 23, 1916	Som	Russia	Aaland strait	Collision; m/s SS Angermanland	?
July 30, 1916	Giacinto Pullino	Italy	Galiola Island	Ran aground, recovered; sank in tow	0
Aug 15, 1916	E.41	UK	Off Harwich	Collision; s/m E.4	15
Aug 15, 1916	E.4	UK	Off Harwich	Collision; s/m E.41	30
Aug 1916	UB-44	Germany	Mediterranean	Op loss; cause unknown	19
Sep 1916	Bremen	Germany	Off Norway	Op loss; cause unknown	30
Oct 9, 1916	Dykkeren	Denmark	Off Copenhagen	Collision; m/s SS Vesla	1
Nov 5, 1916	U-20	Germany	Danish coast	Ran aground	0
Nov 14, 1916	No 4	Japan	Kure	Petrol explosion	2
Dec 7, 1916	UB-46	Germany	Black Sea	Op loss; possible mine	20
Jan 19, 1917	E.36	UK	North Sea	Collision; s/m E.43	31
Jan 19, 1917	E.43	UK	North Sea	Collision; s/m E.36	0
Jan 29, 1917	K.13	UK	Gareloch	Diving error; vent open	32
Feb 14, 1917	F.8	Italy	Off La Spezia	Sank during trials	u/k
Feb 25, 1917	UB-30	Germany	Walcheren	Ran aground; interned	0
Mar 12, 1917	UB-6	Germany	Voorne Island	Ran aground	0
Mar 17, 1917	A.10	UK	Ardrossan	Foundered alongside depot ship	0
Mar 19, 1917	UB-25	Germany	Kiel	Collision; warship	16
April 15, 1917	A.5 (SS-6)	USA	Cavite, Philippines	Slow leak in ballast tank	0
April 16, 1917	C.16	Britain	North Sea off Harwich	Collision; warship	0
April 1917	U-30	Austria-Hungary	Mediterranean	Op loss; cause unknown	21
July 26, 1917	UC-61	Germany	Off Cap Griz Nez	Ran aground; scuttled	1
Aug 1, 1917	W.4	Italy	Mediterranean	Op loss; cause unknown	22
Aug 10, 1917	Delfin	Russia	Murmansk harbor	Collision; foundered	?
Sep 14, 1917	D.2	USA	New London	Sank at dockside	0
Sep 16, 1917	G.9	UK	Norwegian Sea	Collision; HMS Petard	30
Sep 16, 1917	UC-45	Germany	North Sea	Diving failure	0
Oct 28, 1917	C.32	UK	Gulf of Riga	Grounded; blown up by crew	0
Oct 29, 1917	U-52	Germany	Kiel dockyard	Torpedo explosion	5
Nov 17, 1917	K.1	UK	North Sea	Collision; s/m K.4; sunk by friendly gunfire	0
Nov 24, 1917	U-48	Germany	Goodwin Sands	Ran aground; sunk by friendly gunfire	0
Dec 6, 1917	UC-69	Germany	Off Barfleur	Collision; s/m U-96	11
Dec 17, 1917	F.1 (SS-20)	USA	Off Pt Loma, CA	Collision; s/m F.3 (SS-22)	19
Jan 14, 1918	G.8	UK	North Sea	Op loss; cause unknown	31
Feb 1, 1918	K.4	UK	Firth of Forth	Collision; s/m K.6	55
Feb 1, 1918	K.17	UK	Firth of Forth	Collision; cruiser HMS Fearless	48
Feb 11, 1918	Diane	France	Off La Pallice	Explosion	43
April 28, 1918	Prairial	France	Off Le Havre	Collision; SS Tropic	19
July 9, 1918	U-10	Austria	Adriatic	Wrecked	0
July 14, 1918	UB-65	Germany	English Channel	Op loss; cause unknown	37
Aug 2, 1918	Florial	France	Off Salonika	Collision	0
Sep 5, 1918	UC-91	Germany	Baltic	Collision; SS Alexandra Woermann	17
Oct 6, 1918	C.12	UK	Immingham	Collision; destroyer; sank	0
Oct 21, 1918	UB-89	Germany	Off Kiel	Collision; cruiser Frankfurt	7
Nov 18, 1918	U-165	Germany	River Weser	Collision (no other details)	0
Nov 22, 1918	G.11	UK	Northumberland coast	Wrecked	2
Feb 10, 1919	UC-91	Germany	North Sea	Foundered (see Note A)	17
June 2, 1919	Rucumilla	Chile	Off Talcahuana	Human error; diving	0
July 30, 1919	Tuna (SS-27)	USA	Long Island Sound	Foundered; decommissioned	3
Oct 18, 1919	H.41	UK	Blyth	Collision; HMS Vulcan; sank	0
Jan 20, 1920	K.5	UK	WSW of Scillies	Op loss; cause unknown	57
Mar 24, 1920	H.1 (SS-28)	USA	Magdalen Bay, CA	Grounded; sank when refloated	4
Sep 1, 1920	S.5 (SS-11)	USA	Off Cape May, NJ	Human error	0
June 25, 1921	K.15	UK	Portsmouth Dockyard	Hydraulic failure	0

DATE	SUBMARINE	COUNTRY	LOCATION	CAUSE	DIED
Sep 26, 1921	R.6 (SS-82)	USA	San Pedro, CA	Torpedo tubes open; human error	2
Oct 1921	O.8	Neth	Den Helder	Sea cock open; human error	0
Dec 7, 1921	S.48 (SS-159)	USA	Long Island Sound	Human error; manhole cover open	0
Mar 23, 1922	H.42	UK	Off Gibraltar	Collision; HMS Versatile	26
July 17, 1923	S.38 (SS-143)	USA	Anchorage Bay, Alaska	Flooded at mooring; human error	0
Aug 18, 1923	L.9	UK	Hong Kong harbor	Foundered in typhoon	0
Aug 21, 1923	Ro-31	Japan	Off Kobe	Human error; hatch opened when submerged	88
Oct 28, 1923	O.5 (SS-66)	USA	Limon Bay, Canal Zone	Collision; SS Abangarez	3
Oct 29, 1923	Ro-52	Japan	Kure harbor	Tubes opened in error	0
Jan 10, 1924	L.24	UK	SW of Portland Bill	Collision; HMS Resolution	43
Mar 19, 1924	Ro-25	Japan	Off Sasebo	Collision; IJN Tatsuta	46
Jan 13, 1925	S.19 (SS-124)	USA	Nauset, Mass	Ran aground	0
Jan 29, 1925	S.48 (SS-159)	USA	Off Portsmouth, NH	Ran aground	0
Aug 6, 1925	Veniero	Italy	Off Cape Passero (Sicily)	Collision; SS Capena	54
Sep 25, 1925	S.51 (SS-162)	USA	Off Block Island	Collision; liner, SS City of Rome	33
Nov 12, 1925	M.1	UK	Off Start Point	Collision; SS Vidar	69
Aug 9, 1926	H.29	UK	Devonport Dockyard	Flooded; open hatch	6
July 12, 1927	S.4 (SS-109)	USA	Off Cape Cod	Collision; USCGC Paulding	40
Aug 6, 1928	F.14	Italy	Off Brioni island	Collision; destroyer, Missouri	27
Oct 3, 1928	Ondine	France	Off Vigo	Collision; m/s	43
Jan 1929	L.5	UK	Off Portsmouth	Hit by dredger; saved	0
July 9, 1929	H.47	UK	Off Pembroke	Collision; s/m L.12	21
July 9, 1929	L.12	UK	Off Pembroke	Collision; s/m H.47	3
May 11, 1931	Nereus	Greece	Off Pyrgos	Misunderstood order; flooding	41
May 22, 1931	Rabotchi	USSR	100nm SE Helsingfors	Collision; another s/m	39
June 9, 1931	Poseidon	UK	20nm off Wei Hai Wei	Collision; m/s	20
Oct 24, 1931	L.55	USSR	W of Leningrad	Collision; m/s	50
Jan 26, 1932	M.2	UK	West Bay, Portland	Hangar door opened	60
July 8, 1932	Prométhée	France	Off Cherbourg	Hydraulic failure	66
July 23, 1935	Tovarich	USSR	Gulf of Finland	Collision; battleship Murat	55
Nov 20, 1936	U-18	Germany	Bight of Lubeck	Collision tender	8
Nov 1937	M-type	USSR	u/k	Rumor; no firm details	?
Feb 2, 1939	I-63	Japan	Off Bungo Suido	Collision; s/m I-60	81
May 23, 1939	Squalus (SS-192)	USA	Off Isle of Shoals	Induction valve failure	26
June 1, 1939	Thetis	UK	Liverpool Bay	Flooded; human error	99
June 15, 1939	Phenix	France	Off Indo-China coast	Op loss; cause unknown	71
July 24, 1939	Sch-424	USSR	Off Murmansk	Collision	40
Jan 30/31, 1940	U-15	Germany	Baltic	Collision; MTB Iltis	25
Mar 6, 1940	O.11	Neth	Off Den Helder	Rammed by naval tug	3
April 29, 1940	Unity	UK	Off River Tyne	Collision; m/s	4
June 15, 1940	Macallé	Italy	Red Sea	Ran aground; abandoned	0
June 21, 1940	U-122	Germany	Off Hebrides, Scotland	Op loss; cause unknown	48
Aug 29, 1940	I.67	Japan	Off Bonin Island	Op loss; cause unknown	89
Sep 3, 1940	U-57	Germany	Brunsbüttel	Collision; m/s SS Rona	6
Oct 1940	Foca	Italy	Eastern Mediterranean	Op loss; cause unknown	60
Nov 29, 1940	U-104	Germany	SSE of Rockall	Op loss; cause unknown	48
Nov 1940	D.1	USSR	Arctic	Human error; flooded	?
Dec 17, 1940	U-43	Germany	Lorient, France	Sank alongside; human error	0
Mar 7, 1941	U-47	Germany	Atlantic	Op loss; cause unknown	44
June 20, 1941	O.9 (SS-70)	USA	Off Isle of Shoals	Foundered	33
July 19, 1941	Umpire	UK	Off the Wash, UK	Collision with trawler	22
Sep 29, 1941	U-579	Germany	Baltic	Fire in torpedo room	2
Sep 1941	Malaspina	Italy	North Atlantic	Op loss; cause unknown	57
Sep 1941	Smeraldo	Italy	Central Mediterranean	Op loss; cause unknown	45
Oct 2, 1941	I-61	Japan	Off Iki Island	Collision; gunboat	70
Nov 11, 1941	U-580	Germany	Off Memel	Collision; ms/ SS Angelburg	12
Nov 15, 1941	U-583	Germany	Baltic	Collision; s/m U-153	45
Nov 30, 1941	U-206	Germany	Bay of Biscay	Op loss; cause unknown	48
Nov 1941	Marconi	Italy	North Atlantic	Op loss; cause unknown	57
Dec 16, 1941	U-557	Germany	SW of Crete	Collision; s/m Orione (Italian)	43
Dec 17, 1941	Ro-66	Japan	Wake Island	Collision; Ro-62	56
Dec 24, 1941	H.31	UK	Bay of Biscay	Op loss; cause unknown	22
Dec 29, 1941	Ro-60	Japan	Kwajalein Atoll	Ran aground	0
Jan 20, 1942	S.36 (SS-141)	USA	Taka Bakong Reef	Wrecked	0
Jan 24, 1942	S.26 (SS-131)	USA	Gulf of Panama	Collision; PC-460	38
Feb 18, 1942	Surcouf	France	Gulf of Mexico	Op loss; possible collision SS Thompson Lykes	159
Feb 1942	I-23	Japan	Off Hawaii	Op loss; cause unknown	96
March 14, 1942	U-133	Germany	Mediterranean	Op loss; cause unknown	48

DATE	SUBMARINE	COUNTRY	LOCATION	CAUSE	DIED
April 3, 1942	U-702	Germany	North Sea	Op loss; cause unknown	45
June 7, 1942	Veniero	Italy	Western Mediterranean	Op loss; cause unknown	57
June 19, 1942	S.27 (SS-132)	USA	Amchitka Island	Ran aground	0
July 14, 1942	Atilay	Turkey	Off Cannakalle	Diving accident; cause u/k	39
Aug 6, 1942	U-612	Germany	Baltic	Collision; s/m U-444	2
Aug 1942	Grunion (SS-215)	USA	Off Kiska, Aleutians	Op loss; cause unknown	80
Aug 13, 1942	S.39 (SS-144)	USA	Off Rossel Island	Wrecked	0
Sep 2, 1942	U-222	Germany	Off Danzig	Collision; s/m U-626	42
Sep 4, 1942	Sjöbborren	Sweden	Baltic	Collision; m/s	1
Sep 27, 1942	U-165	Germany	Bay of Biscay	Op loss; cause unknown	44
Sep 1942	U-253	Germany	Off Jan Mayen Island	Op loss; cause unknown	48
Oct 11, 1942	U-116	Germany	Bay of Biscay	Op loss; cause unknown	52
Oct 13, 1942	L.16	USSR	Off W coast of USA	Sunk in error; Japanese s/m	55
Oct 1942	I-22	Japan	Solomon Islands	Op loss; cause unknown	95
Nov 5, 1942	U-132	Germany	Atlantic	Op loss; cause unknown	44
Nov 20, 1942	U-184	Germany	North Atlantic	Op loss; cause unknown	48
Nov 1942	I-15	Japan	S of Guadalcanal	Op loss; cause unknown	101
Dec 8, 1942	U-254	Germany	ESE Cape Farewell	Collision; s/m U-221; then sunk by US aircraft	41
1942	Zoea	Italy	Taranto	Sank at mooring	0
Jan 22, 1943	U-553	Germany	North Altantic	Op loss; cause unknown	47
Feb 10, 1943	U-519	Germany	N of Azores	Op loss; cause unknown	50
Feb 15, 1943	U-529	Germany	North Atlantic	Op loss; cause unknown	48
Feb 21, 1943	U-623	Germany	N of Azores	Op loss; cause unknown	46
Feb 24, 1943	Vandal	UK	Off Isle of Arran	Diving failure cause u/k	37
Feb 24, 1943	U-649	Germany	Baltic	Collision; s/m U-232	36
March 19, 1943	U-5	Germany	West of Pilau	Diving accident	21
March 23, 1943	Delfino	Italy	Taranto	Collision pilot boat	u/k
April 14, 1943	Ulven	Sweden	Off Marstrand	Sunk by mine	3
April 23, 1943	U-602	Germany	Mediterranean, off Oran	Op loss; cause unknown	48
April 1943	U-242	Germany	Irish Sea	Op loss; cause unknown	48
May 4, 1943	U-659	Germany	W of Cap Finisterre	Collision; s/m U-439	44
May 4, 1943	U-439	Germany	W of Cap Finisterre	Collision; s/m U-639	40
May 8, 1943	U-663	Germany	Atlantic	Op loss; cause unknown	49
May 9, 1943	U-209	Germany	Atlantic	Op loss; cause unknown	48
May 30, 1943	Untamed	UK	W coast Scotland	Equipment failure	37
June 12, 1943	R.12 (SS-89)	USA	Off Key West	Foundered	42
Jun 1943	I-178	Japan	Off Australian coast	Op loss; cause unknown	88
July 14, 1943	I-179	Japan	Iyo Nada	Op loss; cause unknown	88
July 30, 1943	U-647	Germany	Iceland Gap	Op loss; cause unknown	48
July 1943	Ro-103	Japan	Bismarck Islands	Op loss; cause unknown	38
Aug 5, 1943	U-34	Germany	W of Memel	Collision; depot ship Lech	4
Aug 12, 1943	Illern	Sweden	Kalmarsund Strait	Collision; m/s	1
Aug 21, 1943	U-670	Germany	Baltic	Collision; target ship Bolkoburg	21
Aug 1943	I-25	Japan	Off Espiritu Santo Island	Op loss; cause unknown	101
Sep 8, 1943	U-983	Germany	N of Loba	Collision; U-988	5
Sep 20, 1943	U-346	Germany	Danzig Bay	Diving accident; possible sabotage	37
Sep 23, 1943	M-51	USSR	Off Ochemire	Sunk by accident	u/k
Sep 1943	Grayling (SS-209)	USA	Pacific	Op loss; cause unknown	60
Nov 18, 1943	U-718	Germany	Baltic; N of Bornholm	Collision; s/m U-476	43
Nov 20, 1943	U-768	Germany	Baltic	Collision; s/m U-745	0
Nov 1943	I-21	Japan	Off Gilbert Islands	Op loss; cause unknown	101
Dec 28, 1943	Axum	Italy	W coast of Morea	Grounded	0
Dec 1943	Capelin (SS-289)	USA	Celebes Sea	Op loss; cause unknown	60
1943	Morosini	Italy	Bay of Biscay	Op loss; cause unknown	57
Jan 19, 1944	U-263	Germany	Bay of Biscay	Op loss; cause unknown	56
Jan 1944	U-377	Germany	Atlantic	Op loss; cause unknown	48
Jan 1944	U-972	Germany	North Atlantic	Op loss; cause unknown	50
Feb 14, 1944	U-738	Germany	Off Gdynia	Collision; m/s SS Erna	24
Feb 18, 1944	U-7	Germany	W of Pilau	Diving accident	26
March 16, 1944	Stonehenge	UK	Off Nicobar Islands	Op loss; cause unknown	48
March 17, 1944	U-1013	Germany	Baltic	Collision; s/m U-286	25
March 17, 1944	U-28	Germany	Neustadt	Sank at jetty	1
March 26, 1944	Tullibee (SS-284)	USA	N of Pilau	Own torpedo	79
March 1944	U-851	Germany	Atlantic	Op loss; cause unknown	70
April 4, 1944	I-169	Japan	Truk	Flooded; sank in harbor; error	u/k
April 6, 1944	U-455	Germany	Off La Spezia	Op loss; cause unknown	51
April 8, 1944	U-2	Germany	W of Pilau	Collision; fishing boat Fröse	17
May 15, 1944	U-1234	Germany	Off Gydnia	Collision; tug, Anton	13
May 19, 1944	U-1015	Germany	W of Pilau	Collision; s/m U-1014	36

DATE	SUBMARINE	COUNTRY	LOCATION	CAUSE	DIED
June 13, 1944	I-33	Japan	Inland Sea	Lost on sea trials; cause unknown	92
June 21, 1944	U-441	Germany	English Channel	Op loss; cause unknown	58
Aug 1944	U-180	Germany	Off African coast	Op loss; cause unknown	48
Sep 14, 1944	U-925	Germany	Iceland-Faroes Gap	Op loss; cause unknown	51
Sep 18, 1944	U-1054	Germany	Off Hela	Collision; ferry Peter Wessel	0
Sep 21, 1944	P.402a	USSR	Barents Sea	Sunk in error; Soviet aircraft	38
Sep 22, 1944	U-703	Germany	E of Iceland	Op loss; cause unknown	56
Sep 1944	U-743	Germany	W of Hebrides	Op loss; cause unknown	50
Sep 1944	U-855	Germany	Norwegian Sea	Op loss; cause unknown	56
Sep 1944	U-865	Germany	Norwegian Sea	Op loss; cause unknown	59
Oct 10, 1944	U-2331	Germany	Baltic	Lost in training	15
Oct 21, 1944	U-957	Germany	Lofoten Islands	Collision; pack-ice	0
Oct 24, 1944	U-673	Germany	N of Stavangar	Collision; s/m U-382	0
Oct 24, 1944	Tang (SS-306)	USA	NW of Formosa	Own torpedo	51
Oct 24, 1944	Darter (SS-227)	USA	Bombay shoal	Navigation error; ran aground	0
Oct 1944	I-26	Japan	E of Leyte	Op loss; cause unknown	94
Oct 1944	Escolar (SS-294)	USA	Yellow Sea	Op loss; cause unknown	60
Oct 1944	I-46	Japan	East of Leyte	Op loss; cause unknown	101
Nov 4, 1944	U-1226	Germany	Off Cape Cod	Op loss; cause unknown	61
Nov 8, 1944	Growler (SS-215)	USA	South China Sea	Op loss; cause unknown	80
Nov 14, 1944	U-2508	Germany	Kattegat	Dived with diesel air-intake open	57
Nov 28, 1944	U-80	Germany	Off Hela	Diving accident in training	48
Nov 30, 1944	U-196	Germany	Sunda Strait, Far East	Op loss; cause unknown	57
Nov 1944	U-1226	Germany	Off US East Coast	Op loss; cause unknown	56
Dec 12, 1944	U-479	Germany	Gulf of Finland	Op loss; cause unknown	51
Dec 18, 1944	U-1209	Germany	Wolf Rock	Wrecked; scuttled	10
Dec 19, 1944	U-737	Germany	Vestfjord	Collision; minesweeper MRS-25	31
Jan 7, 1945	U-650	Germany	English Channel	Op loss; cause unknown	47
Jan 1945	I-12	Japan	Central Pacific	Op loss; cause unknown	100
Jan 1945	U-1020	Germany	Off Dornoch Firth, Scotland	Op loss; cause unknown	50
Feb 4, 1945	U-745	Germany	Gulf of Finland	Op loss; cause unknown	48
Feb 12, 1945	U-327	Germany	English Channel	Op loss; cause unknown	44
Feb 15, 1945	U-1053	Germany	Off Bergen	Deep diving test. (see Note B)	45
Feb 18, 1945	U-2344	Germany	Off Heiligendamm	Collision; s/m U-2336	6
March 15, 1945	Lancetfish (SS-296)	USA	Boston	Torpedo tube doors left open; foundered in dock	0
Mar 1945	Kete (SS-369)	USA	Midway-Colnett Strait	Op loss; cause unknown	87
Mar 1945	U-1021	Germany	English Channel	Op loss; cause unknown	50
Mar 1945	U-1169	Germany	English Channel	Op loss; cause unknown	50
April 14, 1945	U-1206	Germany	Off Peterhead	Flooded; human error	3
April 23, 1945	U-398	Germany	Off Scottish coast	Op loss; cause unknown	45
April 30, 1945	U-1055	Germany	English Channel	Op loss; cause unknown	49
April 1945	U-246	Germany	British waters	Op loss; cause unknown	48
May 19, 1945	U-548	Germany	North Atlantic	Op loss; cause unknown	59
July 8, 1945	O.19	Neth	S China Sea	Wrecked	0
June 27, 1946	C.4	Spain	Off Balearic Islands	Collision; destroyer	46
Dec 5, 1946	Ex U-2326	France	Off Toulon	Diving; cause u/k	26
Aug 26, 1949	Cochino (SS-345)	USA	Off N Norway	Battery explosion; foundered	1+6
Jan 12, 1950	Truculent	UK	Thames estuary	Collision tanker	64
April 16, 1951	Affray	UK	N of Alderney	Fractured snorkel	75
Sep 23, 1952	Sibylle	France	Off Toulon	British S-class; cause unknown	44
April 4, 1953	Dumlupinar	Turkey	Dardanelles	Collision; m/s SS Naboland	81
Feb 21, 1955	Pomodon (SS-486)	USA	San Francisco Navy Yard	Hydrogen explosion	5
June 16, 1955	Sidon	UK	Portland harbor	Torpedo explosion	13
July 27, 1955	Sælen	Denmark	Copenhagen	Serious fire	?
Sep 26, 1957	M-256	USSR	Baltic, off Talinn	Sank after flooding to put out fire	35
May 30, 1958	Stickleback (SS-415)	USA	SW of Pearl Harbor	Collision; destroyer	0
May 19, 1959	S-99	USSR	u/k	Explosion at 80m, but surfaced	?
Dec 1959	No.418	China	u/k	Sunk; some crew escaped through torpedo tubes	39
May 2, 1960	Laubie	France	Mediterranean	Collision; m/s SS Ville de Marseille II	0
June 14, 1960	Sargo (SSN-583)	USA	Pearl Harbor	Fire and explosion	1
Jan 27, 1961	S-80	USSR	u/k	Cause unknown	68
July 44, 1961	K-19	USSR	u/k	Nuclear leak; towed home	10
June 1962	K-3	USSR	u/k	Fire, nuclear leak	0
April 10, 1963	Thresher (SSN-589)	USA	E of Boston	Diving trials; cause unknown	129
Aug 27, 1963	Grayback (SSG-577)	USA	Pacific	Electrical fire	1
Feb 12, 1965	K-11	USSR	Severodvinsk	Severe reactor fault	?
Sep 14, 1966	Hai	Germany	North Sea	Foundered in storm	19
Sep 8, 1967	K-3	USSR	Atlantic	Fire	39

DATE	SUBMARINE	COUNTRY	LOCATION	CAUSE	DIED
Nov 3, 1968	Tiru (SS-416)	USA	Frederick Reef	Grounded	0
Jan 25, 1968	Dakar	Israel	E Mediterranean	Disappeared; cause unknown	69
Jan 27, 1968	Minerve	France	W Mediterranean	Disappeared; cause unknown	52
Feb 1968	S-74	USSR	u/k	Sank	52
April 11, 1968	K-129	USSR	NW of Hawaii	Internal explosion	86
May 21, 1968	Scorpion (SSN-589)	USA	SW of Azores	Sank; cause unknown	99
Aug 24, 1968	K-27	USSR	Off Okinawa	Major reactor accident	9
1968	Echo II	USSR	Off Kola Peninsula	Propulsion failure	90
Nov 15, 1969	K-19	USSR	White Sea	Collision; s/m USS Gato	?
Nov 15, 1969	Gato (SSN-615)	USA	White Sea	Collision; s/m K-19	0
Feb 12, 1970	Auriga	UK	Off Gibraltar	Battery explosion; 10 hurt	0
March 4, 1970	Eurydice	France	E of Toulon	Cause unknown	57
April 12, 1970	K-8	USSR	Atlantic, SW Land's End	Fire	52
June 20, 1970	Tautog (SSN-639)	USA	Pacific	Collision; s/m K-108	0
June 20, 1970	K-108	USSR	Pacific	Collision; s/m Tautog	0
July 1, 1971	Artemis	UK	Gosport	Human error; sank at moorings	0
July 29, 1971	Alliance	UK	Portland	Battery explosion; no casualties	0
Feb 24, 1972	K-19	USSR	North Atlantic	Fire	29
Oct 11, 1972	Sirene	France	L'Orient	Faulty torpedo tube	0
June 13, 1973	K-56	USSR	Near Nakhodka	Collision; research ship, Akademik Berg.	27
Aug 28, 1976	K-22	USSR	Ionian Sea	Collision; USS Voge (destroyer)	0
Sep 26, 1976	K-47	USSR	Atlantic	Fire	8
Jan 2, 1977	SX-404 (midget)	Pakistan	Off Karachi	Op loss; cause unknown	8
Dec 31, 1977	Echo II	USSR	Indian Ocean	Fire; surfaced; towed to Vladivostok	?
May 14, 1978	Darter (SS-576)	USA	Western Pacific	Engine room flooded; snorkel valve failure	0
Aug 19, 1978	K-116	USSR	Atlantic (near Rockall)	Nuclear problem; towed home	?
Sep 19, 1979	Tonijn	Neth	Atlantic	Engine room fire; towed to Gibraltar	0
1979	K-45	USSR	u/k	Underwater fire; disabled	?
1979	K-10	USSR	Pacific	Underwater collision	?
Aug 21, 1980	K-122	USSR	100 miles east of Okinawa	Severe engine room problem; fire; towed to Vladivostok	9
April 9, 1981	George Washington (SSBN-508)	USA	South China Sea	Collision with Nissho Maru (Japan), which sank	0
Oct 21, 1981	S-135	USSR	Sweden	Ran aground	0
Oct 24, 1981	S-178	USSR	Off Vladivostok	Collision; m/s	60
Jan 16, 1982	Grayback (SS-574)	USA	Philippine Sea	Diving accident	5
Aug 8, 1982	K-123	USSR	Barents Sea	Coolant leak	
Nov 2, 1982	Victor III	USSR	Caribbean	Fire; towed to Cuba	?
June 23, 1983	K-429	USSR	North Pacific	Sank; open vent; human error	90?
Aug 21, 1983	K-122	USSR	Off Okinawa	Underwater fire	9
Oct 31, 1983	Victor III	USSR	Caribbean	Possible collision with US sonar array; towed home	0
Feb 20, 1984	Romeo-class	N Korea	Korean waters	Sank; cause unknown	56
June 18, 1984	K-131	USSR	Barents Sea	Fire	13
Aug 11, 1984	Nathaniel Greene (SSBN-636)	USA	Irish Sea	Lost propeller; to Holy Loch using stand-by propulsion	0
Sep 18, 1984	Victor I	USSR	Straits of Gibraltar	Collision; Soviet tanker	0
Oct 6, 1986	K-219	USSR	E of Bermuda	Internal explosion; scuttled	4
1987	u/k	China	u/k	Sank; some crew escaped through torpedo tube	?
April 24, 1988	Bonefish (SS-582)	USA	Caribbean	Hydrogen gas explosion during recharging	3
Aug 26, 1988	Pacocha	Peru	Off Peruvian coast	Collision with Japanese trawler	8
April 7, 1989	K-278	USSR	Off Norwegian coast	Electrical fire; explosion	42
Jun 25, 1989	K-192	USSR	Barents Sea	Radiation accident	u/k
Sep 27, 1991	Typhoon	USSR	Arctic	Missile mis-launch	u/k
Feb 11, 1992	Barracuda	Russia	Off Kildin Island	Collision USS Baton Rouge	u/k
Feb 11, 1992	(SSN-689)	Baton Rouge USA		Collision Barracuda (see Note C)	0
May 13, 2000	Kursk	Russia	Arctic Ocean	Torpedo explosion	118
Feb 9, 2001	Greeneville (SSN-772)	USA	Off Hawaii	Collision with Japanese civil ship, Ehime Maru (see Note D)	0
May 3, 2003	No. 361	China	Off Neichangshan Islands	Snorkel fault (?); asphyxiation	70
Oct 5, 2004	Chicoutimi	Canada	Atlantic	Fire	1

Notes **A.** UC-91 sank on September 5, 1918, with the loss of 17 lives but was raised the next day, repaired and returned to service. She then sank for a second (and final) time on February 5, 1919.

B. This loss remains a mystery; why an elderly Type VII should have been conducting a deep-diving test at this very late stage of the war has never been explained.

C. There was no known loss of life. Both boats returned to base but never returned to service.

D. There was no loss of life aboard Greeneville; Ehime Maru sank; 9 people aboard died.

PART VI: SEARCH & RESCUE

Left: A U.S. Navy SSN proceeds to sea with a Deep
Submergence Rescue Vehicle (DSRV) mounted on its
afterdeck. Methods of search and rescue have developed
enormously in the past thirty years, with the emphasis now
strongly on taking the rescue vessel to the stricken
submarine rather than the submariners conducting individual
escapes and being saved once they are on the surface.

PART VI: SEARCH & RESCUE

By the year 2005 and after more than a hundred years of submarine operations, well over 200 submarines had suffered accidents in which lives had been lost. These disasters were the result of collisions with surface ships or other submarines, grounding, fire, explosion, design faults, or human error, due to genuine mistakes or through neglect on the part of their crews, or, in some cases, dockyard workers.

HUMAN LIMITATIONS

The design and construction of submarines have improved dramatically over the past century, as have the methods of locating them when sunk and of recovering them. But the one factor that has not changed one iota is man himself. To survive, the human body must inhale air that is composed of nitrogen (78 percent), oxygen (21 percent), argon (0.94 percent) and carbon dioxide (0.04 percent). Of these, it is

the intake of oxygen that is essential to life (the nitrogen and argon have no known function in the process), following which the waste products—carbon dioxide (CO_2) plus some moisture—are exhaled. In an open environment (i.e., the atmosphere) this process continues naturally. But when a submarine sinks the volume automatically becomes sealed and if, as will almost certainly be the case, one or more compartments are flooded, the volume will be correspondingly reduced. The surviving crew members then withdraw into the unflooded compartments, where they cannot help but consume the lesser amount of oxygen and exhale a proportionally greater amount of CO_2. Then, unless something can be done to alleviate the situation, the survivors will suffer a succession of symptoms which will start with shortness of breath and then pass through reduced mental alertness, headaches, dizziness and vomiting, to unconsciousness

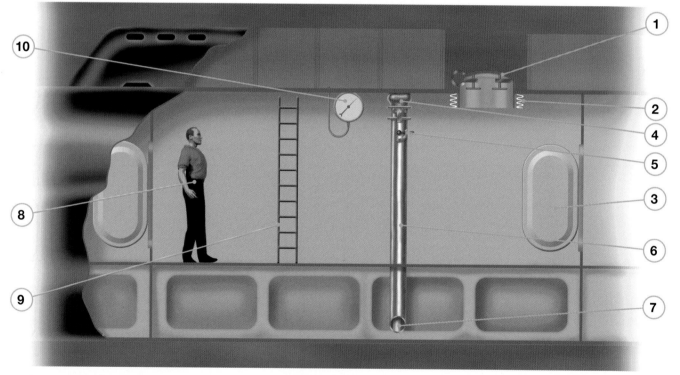

Twill Trunk (Submerged Submarine)

A submerged submarine with an access hatch (1), secured by screw-clips and fitted with the Twill Trunk escape system (2). This Twill Trunk is made of rubberized cotton-twill reinforced with steel hoops, enabling it to be stowed as here, concertina-fashion, around a circular steel skirt, which protects it when the hatch is in normal use.

At the highest point of the hull is a flood valve (4), backed up by a flap valve (5), allowing, when opened, water to flow into a large tube (6), which follows the contour of the hull down to the bilges (7).

The ladder that allows access to the trunk is stowed against the side of the hull (9). There is also a differential depth gauge (10) that shows the difference in pressure between inside and outside the compartment. In the case shown here, the compartment is at atmospheric pressure, so the gauge shows the submarine's actual depth. The watertight doors (3) are open. The installation takes up very little space, so the crewmen (8) are able to work and move normally.

Right: A submariner wearing an immersion suit climbs the ladder to the escape chamber. He is faced by a controlled ascent, followed by survival on the surface until a rescue ship finds him.

and, finally, to death. The situation is further complicated by the fact that attempts to limit the damage or to escape require physical exertion, which not only becomes physically more difficult as time passes, but also increases the rate at which oxygen is consumed and CO_2 is generated.

Other gases can have varying effects on the crew. Chlorine gas is a major hazard in diesel-electric submarines, particularly the older ones, since it is released if seawater comes into contact with the sulphuric acid in the batteries, after a collision, for example. Carbon monoxide is a by-product of the internal combustion process and will normally be ejected outboard by the engine exhaust systems, but in the pre-1918 petrol-driven boats it was a definite problem. Hydrogen is generated in large quantities

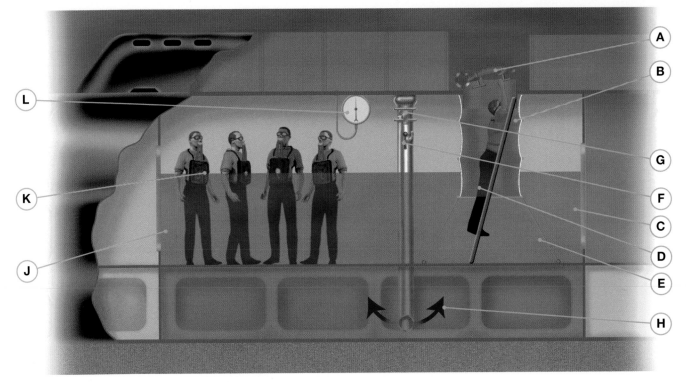

Damaged Submarine at Rest on the Sea Bed

In this scenario, the submarine has been damaged forward and has come to rest on the bottom; preparations for escape are complete. The watertight doors (C) and (J) have been closed, and the Twill Trunk (B) has been extended and lashed (E) in place to eyes on the floor. The valves (F) and (G) have been opened and water has flowed (H) into the space until the pressure is the same as that outside, as marked by the gauge (L). Crewmen are standing in the water up to their chests (K). Each man in turn dons his escape apparatus, ducks under the trunk, and climbs the ladder. He presses the vent in the hatch cover and when the trunk is fully flooded pushes the cover open (A) until he can float upwards and escape. The lid closes behind him, and the cycle starts again.

Although this system was a great step forward, this diagram clearly shows its two major disadvantages. The first was that only one man at a time could escape, the second that the remainder waited in very cold water and in an atmosphere that became increasingly unpleasant.

Left: Trainees look somewhat apprehensive as they wait to test their Deep Sea Escape Apparatus (DSEA) at HMS *Dolphin*, the British submarine training school, in 1929.

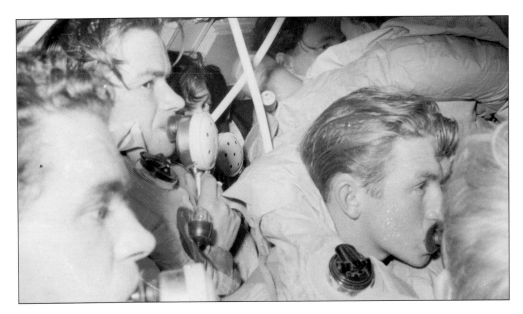

Left: U.S. submariners wearing breathing apparatus are crammed into a tight space as they await being called forward to enter the escape hatch during survival training. They look every bit as anxious as their British comrades-in-arms (opposite), but such training is essential if they are to survive in a real emergency at sea.

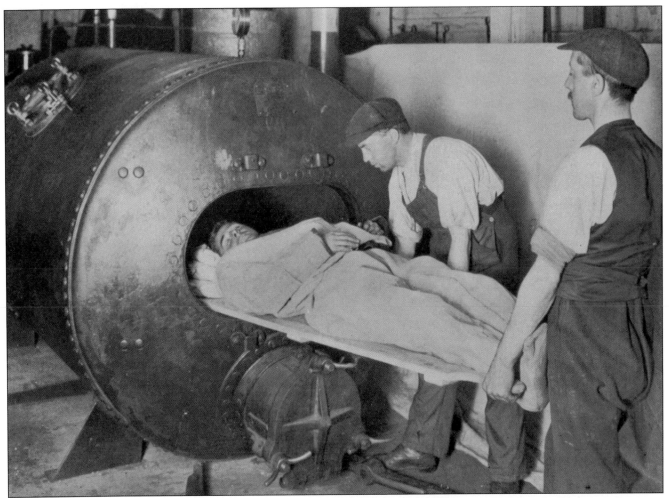

Above: As new problems were encountered, equipment and techniques had to be devised to overcome them. Such processes necessarily included very courageous men to test them, as with this British submariner in the 1930s testing an early decompression chamber.

when the batteries are on charge, although it is not, of itself, poisonous to humans. But, if it is not rapidly and efficiently vented to the atmosphere, pockets will build up within the hull and will almost inevitably be ignited by a spark, causing a very violent explosion.

Another factor for the crew is the cold. Under normal conditions the submarine is heated to produce a comfortable working environment, but an almost inevitable consequence of a mishap is that whatever battery power remains must be conserved for lighting and other life-support functions, so that the submarine rapidly cools to the temperature of the surrounding water, which is about 4 degrees Celsius (39 degrees Fahrenheit).

SEARCHING FOR SUNKEN SUBMARINES

In the early days, the first problem lay in knowing that a submarine was actually missing. Sometimes, as in the case of a collision with a surface ship, the latter might report the

Above: U.S. Navy submariners practice their survival techniques by wearing their Momsen lung breathing apparatus (see page 120), while continuing to operate their equipment.

Below: On a training exercise, two U.S. Navy sailors have found a smoke candle, indicating a distressed submarine (DISSUB) and have rescued a survivor, who is wearing the full protective suit.

Right: Submerged submarines can send simple messages to the surface using colored signals. A single white/yellow candle indicates position, while two white/yellow candles about 3 minutes apart mean, "I am preparing to surface, keep clear." A red grenade means, "I am preparing to surface in emergency; keep clear and prepare to assist."

Above: The U.S. Navy's Scorpio remotely operated vehicle (ROV) is an advanced device capable of many underwater tasks. It is deployed aboard vessels such as the MSC-operated *Edison Chouest* and is used for tasks such as photographing the sunken Japanese ship, *Ehime Maru* (see page 137).

Left: The internationally standardized Type 0070 Submarine Indicator Buoy is released by a distressed submarine and floats to the surface where it displays a bright light, which flashes every two seconds and transmits two separate radio signals at 243 and 406 Megaherz, respectively. The batteries for both light and radios have a life of about 72 hours. The buoy is colored orange.

collision, or the submarine might be seen to be in trouble, as was the case with the U.S. Navy's *S.38*, whose stern was spotted by the passing SS *Alanthus*. Those circumstances apart, the shore authorities had to allow the submarine's expected time of return to pass before instituting any active search.

The next problem was that the area to be searched—even in the early days when submarines seldom ventured far into the open ocean—could be very large. The situation was partially eased when smoke candles came into use for release from a distressed submarine, but submarines carried only a limited stock and there was always a danger that the candles might be expended when there was no surface ship or aircraft in the area to see them. Later, submarine distress buoys came into use; these were released on a cable and contained a telephone link to the distressed submarine, and eventually an automatic radio transmitter as well. In the days before sonar, however, even when a submarine was known to be overdue and the area where it had been operating was reasonably certain, it was frequently the case that the submarine could not be found—as happened in the case of the Australian *AE-1* on September 14, 1914.

RECOVERY OF SUBMARINES

Once the submarine had been located, the problem was what to do next. It had been known since the remarkable escape of Bauer and his crew in 1851 that if survivors

Above: During system trials a British submariner wearing full-body survival equipment, having escaped from a "sunken" submarine, has risen so rapidly that he blasts out of the water on arrival at the surface.

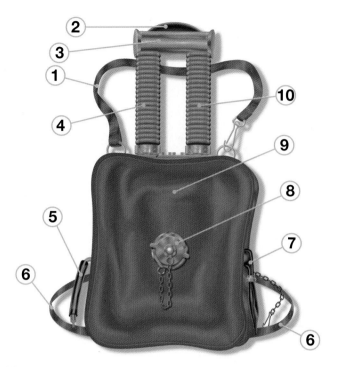

Momsen Lung

The Momsen Lung was designed to clean and reoxygenize the escaper's exhaled air as he was rising from the stricken submarine to the surface. The large rubber bag (9) was suspended from his neck by a strap (1) and secured by a waist strap (6). The escaper was connected to the bag via a mouthpiece (2), valve box (3) and two tubes, one (4) for exhaled carbon dioxide, the other (10) for incoming oxygen. The exhaled carbon dioxide passed into a soda-lime canister (9) inside the bag, the poisonous carbon dioxide was removed. The air then passed through an oxygen replenisher back to the wearer via the second tube and through the valve box and mouthpiece (3). The Momsen Lung also included a connection (5) for coupling to an oxygen cylinder at the escape position, essentially a last-minute top-up before the escaper left the submarine. There was also a relief valve (7) and a connector (8) for extra canisters when the lung was used as protection against smoke or carbon monoxide poisoning. The wearer was also supplied with separate goggles and a nose clip.

waited until the internal and external pressures had equalized then the hatch could be opened allowing the men to float to the surface in the bubble of air. By the time that submarines began to enter service in large numbers in the early 20th Century, however, such individual escapes seemed to have been forgotten and the emphasis was on collective escape. Thus, the response to an accident was to await the arrival of a salvage ship; some navies, such as those of Germany and Russia, even built specialized ships with catamaran hulls to carry out submarine recovery. These would make best speed to the scene, send down divers to locate the boat, and then place chains or cables around the hull so that it could be raised. The transit and the recovery process were inevitably lengthy—at least days and sometimes several weeks—so that the chances of the submarine being recovered while any of the crew were still alive were remote if not non-existent. One successful example was when the Chilean Navy recovered the submarine *Rucumilla*, but in that particular case the submarine was spotted quickly, the salvage ships happened to be located very close by, and the Chilean Navy reacted particularly swiftly.

Following World War One, most major navies developed breathing apparatus to enable individuals to survive the ascent from a sunken submarine to the surface. These included the Momsen Lung (USA), Davis Submerged Escape Apparatus (UK), the Tauchretter or Dräger lung (Germany), and *la bouée Bouteille* (France). It was the U.S. Navy that questioned the value of such devices and pioneered "free escape," in which the submariner has no breathing apparatus at all. This technique is possible because the air which he has inhaled in the sunken submarine is already compressed and as he ascends it expands at a rate proportional to the reduction in pressure; in other words, the survivor always has sufficient air inside him and all he has to do is to open his mouth to exhale surplus air. Such a procedure goes against a man's natural instincts and requires training and practice, which is why there are 100-foot tall towers in naval bases such as Portsmouth in England.

The escapers also required facilities to leave the submarine and there were escape facilities, such as the British Twill Trunk or escape chamber, usually one at each

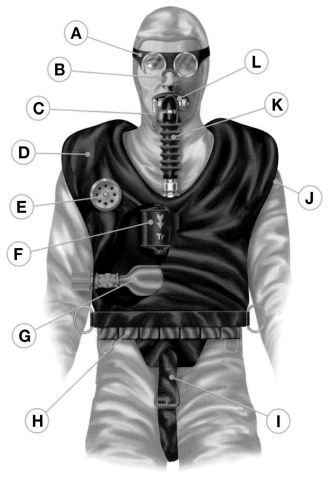

Davis Submerged Escape Apparatus (DSEA)

The DSEA consisted of rubber breathing (3) and buoyancy (12) bags, suspended from a neckstrap (1) and secured by a waistbelt (4). The escaper's mouthpiece (2) was connected to the bag via a single concertina tube leading into the carbon dioxide absorbing canister (8). Suspended below the bag was a steel cylinder (7) containing 56 liters of oxygen at a pressure of 120 atmospheres, provided with a control valve (6), which was linked to the breathing bag by a tube. When the control valve was opened it admitted oxygen to the breathing bag, charging it to a pressure equal to that of the surrounding water, allowing the escaper to breathe normally. The escaper was provided with separate goggles and a nose clip. A speed-retarding vane or apron (9), secured by a cord, had to be released and extended by hand to limit the rate of ascent.

Immediately prior to escaping, the escaper charged his apparatus from a manifold linked to an oxygen cylinder inside the submarine, admitting sufficient oxygen to enable him to breathe comfortably. This tube (10) was fitted to a non-return valve. There was also a non-return release valve (13) on the breathing bag, which released air from the bag as the water pressure decreased during the ascent. On arrival at the surface this valve was closed; the trapped air inside the breathing bag then added to the escaper's buoyancy.

An emergency oxygen supply was provided by two small canisters, known as "oxylets" (11, only one shown), inside the breathing bag. These were activated by grasping the neck and twisting and breaking the seal. The emergency buoyancy bag was inflated before leaving the submarine by means of breaking the seal on a third "oxylet" (5). It could be recharged on the surface, if necessary, by opening the valve on the mouthpiece (14), blowing into it and then re-closing the valve.

Dräger Tauchretter

The Dräger Tauchretter (= diving savior), usually known in English as the "Dräger Lung," was used by German U-boatmen from 1912 to 1945; there were only minor modifications over this period–this illustration shows the Model 1929.

The Tauchretter was essentially a large bifurcated bag (D) (J), open at the front end, which fitted over the wearer's head. To ensure that pressure within the bag was equal to that of the lungs, it was necessary to wear a crotch strap (I) which ensured that it was fitted closely to the wearer's torso. The mouthpiece (L) was linked to the bag via a concertina tube, where the sodium peroxide canister (F) absorbed the exhaled carbon dioxide. The cleansed air was then mixed with oxygen from the cylinder (G) before returning to the wearer. The wearer was required only to breathe in and out normally.

The sodium peroxide and oxygen cylinders required replacing from time to time or after use, and for this purpose the front end of the bag was lined with a series of small brass plates that were secured by pressing them together and locking with a brass clamp (H), thus ensuring an air/watertight seal. The relief valve (E) released air if the pressure became too great when below the surface.

On reaching the surface the wearer closed the valve (K), blew into the bag until it was inflated, and then closed the cock (C), whereupon the bag served as a lifejacket. The wearer was also provided with goggles (A) and a nose clip (B).

Above: U.S. Navy submariner demonstrates the use of the newly invented "lung" and the after escape hatch, during trials in July 1930. The submarine is USS *V-5* (SC-1), later renamed USS *Narwhal* (SS-167).

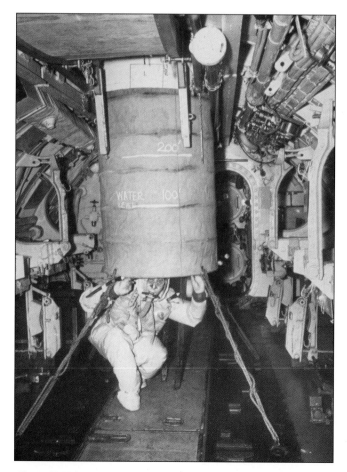

Above: British sailor demonstrates entry to the "Twill Trunk" aboard a Royal Navy submarine in the 1930s. The trunk was normally folded and secured with the leather straps, here seen hanging. Note the depth indication marks.

end of the submarine, from which the survivors could escape in groups of up to four men at a time. There have been reports of escapes having been made through the torpedo tubes, but this is only possible for men who can fit into a 21-inch tube. Also, the last man cannot escape since there is no way in which he can close the inboard door once he is in the torpedo tube.

It is too easy to imagine that once a submariner exits the submarine his survival is guaranteed, but this is unfortunately not the case. A number of deaths have occurred during the ascent. Even when on the surface, if there is no rescue ship at hand, survivors may die of exhaustion or exposure. It is for these reasons that all submariners are now outfitted with exposure suits, and parachute teams are trained to drop to collections of survivors on the surface to enable them to continue to survive until a surface ship arrives.

SUBMARINE RESCUE SHIPS

From early days the most immediate form of rescue has been a surface rescue ship, carrying divers and equipped with grabs, lifting gear, diving bells, decompression chambers, medical facilities and, more recently, remotely operated vehicles (ROVs). There are currently sixteen such ships in service, which are either purpose-built or converted from oil field supply ships. All are very sophisticated and most include facilities such as helicopter landing pads and dynamic positioning, which enables them to "hover" over a precise spot on the seabed. However, they also share a number of common shortcomings. The first is that they are expensive to build and operate, and the second that they take a finite time to travel from their normal station to the scene of the disaster; at a sustained speed of 16 knots, for example, an Auxiliary Submarine Rescue ship (ASR) would take $6^{1}/_{2}$ hours to cover every 100 miles to the scene of the disaster, longer in bad weather. In addition, the ASR's on-site operations may be hampered or even halted by bad weather or heavy seas.

Several navies, including those of Australia, the UK and the USA, have taken an alternative course by planning to use "vessels of opportunity" (VOO) and designing their equipment accordingly. This means maintaining a list of all suitable vessels, maintaining a few on dormant

Right: Japanese DSRV *Angler Fish 2* is lowered through the center of Mother Ship *Chihaya* as part of Exercise Pacific Reach 2002, which involved submarines and rescue ships from five navies and observers from a further six.

Above: Until the appearance of rescue vessels such as the U.S. Navy's DSRV, seen here, the only method of submarine rescue was by individual escape.

contracts, and engaging individual ships for exercises, training and, in the ultimate, for live rescues. When the scheme is activated the nearest suitable VOO sails immediately to the appropriate loading point, loads the rescue vehicle, A-frame, containers housing equipment, control facilities, and the decompression chambers, and then sails for the scene of the disaster. Uniquely, as will be described, the U.S. Navy's Deep Submergence Rescue Vehicles (DSRVs) can deploy aboard rescue submarines.

EMERGENCY LIFE SUPPORT SYSTEMS

Among the problems facing survivors in a sunken submarine are critical deficiencies in certain essential survival stores. To overcome this an "Emergency Life Support System" for supplying critical survival supplies to disabled submarines has been developed. The supplies which might be provided include CO_2 absorbent, oxygen candles, medical supplies, food, and liquids which are packed into a "pod," a small watertight container of

standardized dimensions. Four of these pods are normally placed in a carousel and lowered to the submarine where they are "posted" by a diver through one of the escape hatches or, in certain cases, through an empty torpedo tube. Alternatively they can be delivered by an ROV.

CURRENT SYSTEMS

AUSTRALIA.

Like the UK, Australia employs a civilian contractor to provide its submarine rescue service. The service comprises the Remotely Operated Rescue Vehicle (RORV), named Remora, together with two recompression chambers with the capacity for thirty-six personnel each. Remora can be connected to a transfer chamber for TUP (transfer under pressure) operations and the design is influencing that of the new U.S. system. (It is an "in" joke that REMORA stands for: Really Excellent Method Of Rescuing Australians!)

BRAZIL.

Brazil operates a single Submarine Rescue Ship (ASR), NSS *Felinto Perry.*

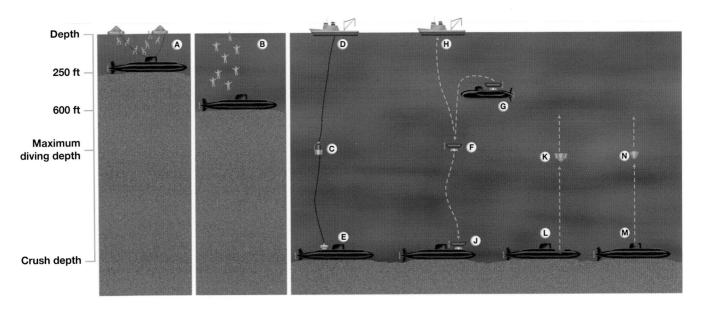

Modern Submarine Rescue

The diagram summarizes various modern means of rescuing the crew from a sunken submarine.

In submarines lying at depths no greater than 250 feet free escapes (A) can be made through the escape hatches. The crew do not have to wear immersion suits, but will require inflatable life rafts on the surface to give them shelter from cold, rain and wind until rescue vessels arrive.

In submarines lying at depths up to 600 feet it is feasible to use the British "free ascent" method (B). Such escapers will wear immersion suits, giving them protection on the surface.

The Rescue Bell (C) is deployed aboard a Mother Ship (D) and winches itself down to the submarine (E) by means of a cable secured to a ring on the submarine's escape hatch (E). This can be put in place by a diver, or in some navies the sunken submarine releases a buoy that lifts the cable to the surface.

A more modern method uses the Deep Submergence Rescue Vehicle (F), a self-propelled submarine that is deployed aboard either a submarine (G) or a Mother Ship (H). A skirt on the underside of the DSRV mates with a standard hatch on the stricken submarine and survivors are then transferred to the DSRV, which takes them to another submarine or Mother Ship. The DSRV shuttles between the two until all the survivors have been rescued.

Finally, there are two variations of the same theme. (K) is the German IKL rescue sphere, as fitted in the Indian Navy's Shishumar-class. It consists of a spherical survival vessel and a large flotation collar. The device is carried in a recess in the submarine's topside (L); entrance is via two hatches in the floor, and exit via a hatch in the roof. The sphere is sized to accommodate the entire crew.

The Russian crew escape system (M) (N) is built into the sail, but appears otherwise similar in concept to the IKL system. It is installed in the Akula- and Sierra II-classes; it was also installed—and used operationally—in the sole Mike-class SSN.

CHINA. The People's Liberation Army (Navy) (PLA(N)) is believed to have built all escape and rescue facilities to the same specifications as those of the RFN (Russian Federation Navy), and since the latter has accepted the relevant Standard NATO Agreement (STANAG) it can be inferred that PLA(N) submarines with a docking seat can receive a Submarine Rescue Vehicle (SRV) fitted with a NATO STANAG rescue skirt. Each of the two fleets of the PLA(N) operates a Dajaing-class Auxiliary Submarine Rescue ship which serves as a Mother ship (MOSHIP), equipped with a Submarine Rescue Chamber (SRC).

ITALY.

Italy has recently introduced the SRV300, built by Drass Galeazzi, which is deployed aboard the dedicated MOSHIP, *Anteo*. This system proved particularly successful during the Exercise "Sorbet Royal 2000." Italy also used the McCann bell system.

Right: The Gabler Rescue Sphere is built into the upper deck of the submarine and accessed directly from the inside of the submarine. It accommodates the entire crew and once on the surface it provides accommodation until rescue vessels arrive.

Above: The Indian Navy's four Shishumar-class submarines are fitted with the Gabler Rescue Sphere. This picture, taken during a live trial of the system, shows the space it normally occupies.

Above: The Japanese Submarine Rescue Service (SRS) operates two of these Japanese-designed and -built Deep Submergence Rescue Vehicles, each of which has a dedicated "Mother Ship" (MOSHIP). They are not air transportable.

INDIA.

The Indian Navy operates a single ASR, INS *Nireeshak*, which is normally based at Mumbai. *Nirseeshak's* equipment includes a ten-man SRC and a two-man Type GK59 SRC, as well as three recompression chambers, each capable of accommodating six survivors. India has also signed a memorandum of understanding with the U.S. Navy concerning submarine rescue.

JAPAN.

The Japanese Submarine Rescue Service consists of two Deep Submergence Rescue Vehicles, each with a dedicated MOSHIP. The system is not air transportable and is limited in area of operations by the speed and range of the MOSHIPs, *Chiyoda* and *Chihaya*.

SOUTH KOREA.

The Korean LR5K rescue chamber is based on the UK design, which itself was adapted for rescue from an offshore submersible built in 1978. The LR5K is operated from a dedicated MOSHIP, *Chung Hae Jin*, which also carries an ROV and a nine-man diving bell.

NATO.

The NATO SRS is a joint project between France, Norway and the UK, with an in-service date of 2007; it is planned that it will play a full role during Exercise "Sorbet Royal 2008." Although termed a NATO system it will, in fact, be owned solely by the three participating nations.

RUSSIA.

The RFN has acceded to the Submarine Escape & Rescue STANAGs, but, so far as is known, no submarines or rescue vehicles have yet been built or modified to these specifications. It is known that a NATO SRV can mate with an RFN disabled submarine (DISSUB) although, since the seating is narrow and small in diameter, extreme care is required. Conversely, the RFN standard skirt is too small to allow an RFN SRV to mate with a NATO DISSUB. The RFN operates one Elberus-class and four Rudnitsky-class ASRs, each of which operates a single SRV. The RFN also operates a number of different classes of small submersibles, some of which must, presumably, be tasked with rescue.

Above: Some modern Russian submarines are fitted with a rescue pod, similar in concept to the Gabler system, but which is mounted in the sail. The V-shaped outline can be seen just abaft the raised mast.

SWEDEN.

The RSwedN operates an SRV designated URF (*U-bats Raddnings Farkost*), which displaces 52 tons and can be operated from a variety of MOSHIPs, although its size and

Below: The Swedish *URF*, commissioned in 1978, has a crew of five, can accommodate 26 survivors (the entire crew of any in-service Swedish submarine), and is road transportable. It is taken to the scene by a dedicated Mother Ship, HSwedMS *Belos*.

weight make it difficult to airlift. It is normally deployed aboard the Swedish dedicated MOSHIP, HSwedMS *Belos*.

SPAIN.

The Spanish navy operates a single MOSHIP, the *Neptuno*, a former oil field supply vessel, which is currently equipped with a submersible, *Vosma*, which will be replaced by a DSRV in due course.

TURKEY.

Turkey operates a Submarine Rescue Ship (ASR), *Kurturan*, which is equipped with a McCann bell. Turkey is also a registered observer in the NATO Submarine Rescue System (NSRS) program with France, Norway and the UK.

UNITED KINGDOM.

The British rescue organization is provided by a civilian contractor, Rumic, which operates a rescue submersible, the LR5, and an associated 25-ton A-frame, which is used to lower and raise the submersible from the water. The system requires a MOSHIP. The LR5 design was based on a vessel developed for the offshore oil and gas industries and was upgraded in 2000; it can now accommodate fifteen survivors. The UK also operates a Scorpio ROV and a SPAG (Submarine Parachute Assistance Group) team, whose main task is to parachute to submarine survivors on the surface so as to support their survival until the arrival of a surface rescue ship.

Above: The British LR5 is 9 ft long, 9.8 ft wide and 9 ft high (without skirt). Total vehicle weight is 21.3 tons and maximum operating depth 1,500 feet.

Above: The entire LR5 system, including the vehicle itself, plus the A-frame, two ISO containers, as well as the operating and support crew, is air transportable in either one Antonov An-124 plus two/three C-130s, or one C-17 plus six C-130s, or two C-17s.

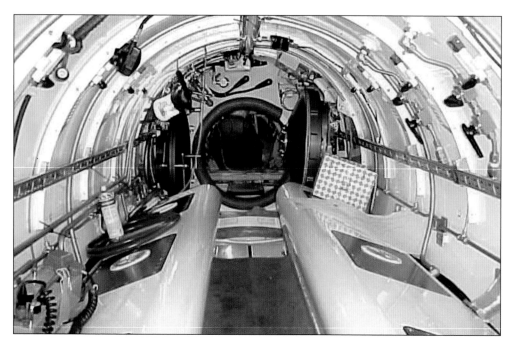

Left: Maximum capacity of LR5 is sixteen survivors and, following a mid-life modernization, it now has a basic transfer-under-pressure (TUP) capability using a deck transfer lock, and Type A and Type B chambers. Vehicle crew comprises one pilot and one diver lock-out chamber operator, and there are eight qualified support staff.

MODERN U.S. NAVY SYSTEMS

The U.S. Navy is currently changing from one system to another, so both are described. The U.S. Navy constructed two Deep Submergence Rescue Vehicles (DSRVs) in the 1960s, but one was mothballed in 1995, leaving just one to meet all commitments, together with two Submarine Rescue Chambers (SRCs), which were built in the 1940s. All these systems are based at the Deep Submergence Center in San Diego, California, and have global mobility using a U.S. Air Force C-5 Galaxy transport aircraft, which flies into a nearby airfield from which the assets are transported by road to a port facility and then carried by either surface ship or submarine to the area of the disabled submarine.

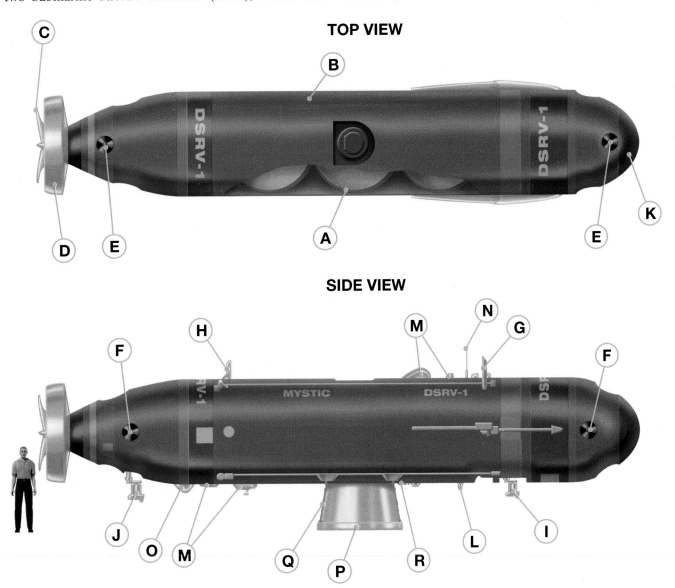

TOP VIEW

SIDE VIEW

Deep Submergence Rescue Vehicle (DSRV)

The U.S. Navy's two DSRVs were designed and built in response to the *Thresher* tragedy. They are 49 ft long, with a beam of 8 ft and submerged displacement of 38 tons. Crew is four (two pilots and two rescue operators), and the capacity is 24 survivors.

There are three pressure valves (A), interconnected by hatches, housed in a streamlined casing (B). Silver/zinc batteries drive a single propeller (C) housed inside a tiltable shroud (D), and four ducted thrusters–two vertical (E) and two horizontal (F). This system enables the DSRV to move or hover in tidal streams of up to 3 knots.

The DSRV is fitted with numerous sensors. The CCTV system has four extendable and steerable pan-and-tilt units: top forward (G), top aft (H), bottom forward (I), and bottom aft (J). There are a forward-looking sonar (K), hydrophones (L), and various sonar arrays (M). Communications include UHF (N) and underwater telephone (O).

On reaching the disabled submarine, the DSRV mates with the hatch on the submarine, using its skirt (P), which is fitted with a shock absorbing system (Q). There is also a manipulator arm, which can lift up to 1,000 lb. On the successful transfer of survivors, the submarine and DSRV close their hatches and the DSRV then returns to the Mother Ship (either a surface vessel or submarine), transfers the men, and then returns to the stricken submarine for more, until all have been rescued.

Left: Today's submarine rescue is a truly international undertaking, as exemplified by this U.S. Navy DSRV being loaded aboard a Ukrainian Antonov An-124, a sight that would have been totally unthinkable during the Cold War.

Below: USS *Tennessee* (SSBN-734) shows two standard escape hatches on her afterdeck (there is another forward of the sail). The dimensions, fittings and markings are defined in a Standard NATO Agreement (STANAG), which has been accepted throughout the world.

DEEP SUBMERGENCE RESCUE VEHICLE (DSRV)

The DSRVs were developed as a direct result of the loss of USS *Thresher* on April 10, 1963, and further by the loss of *Scorpion* on May 21, 1968. These tragedies combined to make it very obvious that there was an urgent need for a capability to rescue the crew of an SSN or SSBN trapped on the sea floor. The design was prepared by Lockheed and it was originally estimated that the needs of the large, globally deployed, Cold War submarine force required twelve DSRVs plus three purpose-built surface mother ships and a number of SSNs modified as mother submarines (MOSUBs). However, the costs of such a program were so astronomical that not even the U.S. Navy could afford them. Therefore, just two DSRVs were built—*Mystic* (DSRV-1), which became operational in 1971, and *Avalon* (DSRV-2), operational from 1972—plus a small number of modified SSNs. The operation of the DSRV is shown in the accompanying diagrams.

A key advantage of the DSRV system was its ability to operate from a submarine MOSHIP, thus freeing itself

Above: Captain Allan R. McCann, U.S. Navy, himself a trained and experienced submariner, invented the McCann Submarine Rescue Chamber.

from the problems faced by a surface ship when it is subjected to bad weather. The DSRVs have also been very effective internationally and have been regularly and very successfully tested with British and French nuclear submarines, in addition to regular exercises with U.S. SSBN/SSNs.

SUBMARINE RESCUE CHAMBER (SRC)

The Submarine Rescue Chamber or "McCann Bell" is an example of technology adapted from the era of the *Squalus* rescue that still works today and is cheap and simple to operate. The United States still operates two, but Turkey is the main operator, with three in service, and Italy also uses the system.

U.S. NAVY SUBMARINE RESCUE DIVING AND RECOMPRESSION SYSTEM (SRDRS)

The DSRV is being replaced in 2006 by the Submarine Rescue Diving and Recompression System (SRDRS), a fully integrated system composed of three elements. The first component is the Assessment/Underwater Work System (AUWS), which consists of Atmospheric Diving Suits (ADS)—also known as "newt suits"—and Remotely Operated Vehicles, together with the associated support package. The AUWS would be the lead element to arrive at the scene, where its first task would be to locate the disabled submarine, assess the actions required and, where necessary, clear the hatch to be used for the rescue. The AUWS would also be responsible for posting the necessary Emergency Life Support Stores (ELSS) pods to the survivors in the DISSUB.

The second element of the SRDRS is the Submarine Decompression System (SDS), which consists of two Submarine Decompression Chambers (SDCs) and their associated support packages.

Left: Machinist's Mate 1st Class Eric Lang conducts pre-dive checks aboard the U.S. Navy's *Mystic* (DSRV-1) during NATO Exercise Sorbet Royal 2000, which took place in the eastern Mediterranean.

Above: This view of a U.S. Navy's DSRV clearly shows the skirt, whose dimensions are also defined by the NATO STANAG and which will mate with any hatch built to the same standard. This enables the DSRV to shuttle between the Mother Submarine (MOSSUB) and the Distressed Submarine (DISSUB).

Right: US Navy survival suit enables submariners to escape from a distressed submarine, ascend to the surface, and then survive until a rescue ship or helicopter arrives.

Submarine Rescue Chamber (SRC)
1. Cable from Mother Ship.
2. Compressed air from Mother Ship.
3. Upper chamber.
4. Compressed air motor.
5. Hatch to lower chamber.
6. Compensating tank.
7. Winch.
8. Ballast tank.
9. Pivoted support for downhaul cable.
10. Lead ballast.
11. Skirt.
12. Downhaul cable (secured to submarine escape hatch).
13. Intake pipe for ballast tank.
14. Lower chamber (open to sea).
15. Water inlet cock.
16. Upper chamber access hatch.
17. Venting hose to Mother Ship.

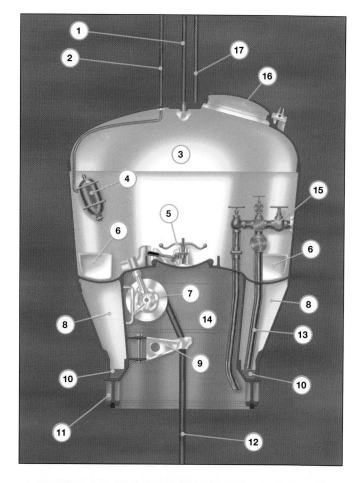

The main components of the SRC consist of a bell housing an upper (3) and lower (14) chamber, and a ballast tank (8). The SRC is permanently connected to the Mother Ship by a cable (1), a compressed air supply pipe (2), and a vent hose (17), and is manned by two operators who enter through the upper recess hatch (16). A diver shackles the downhaul cable (12) to a special lug on the distressed submarine's hatch and the operators then use the winch (7) to pull the SRC downwards until it sits on the deck of the stricken submarine, immediately over the hatch.

With the SRC still held in position by the downhaul cable, the operators then use the compressed air to empty the lower chamber, the water being transferred to the ballast tank (8) to ensure that the SRC remains heavy enough to remain in position and to maintain a watertight seal. The operators then vent the pressure from the lower chamber, via the upper chamber and the venting hose, to the outer atmosphere. When the pressure has been equalized, the lower chamber access hatch (5) is opened and an operator climbs down to release the downhaul cable and open the hatch into the submarine.

The SRC normally accommodates seven passengers, so the first priority is to transfer fresh air to the submarine and vent its foul air, and also to transfer food and clothing for the survivors staying behind to await their turn for rescue. Once this is completed, the first passengers climb into the SRC, the submarine hatch is closed, the downhaul cable re-secured, and the lower chamber hatch is closed. Water is then transferred from the ballast tank back into the lower chamber. Once the SRC is freed from the submarine, the winch on the Mother Ship raises the SRC to the surface, with the downhaul serving as a brake. The SRC then continues to shuttle between the submarine and the surface until all survivors have been rescued.

Right: A tranquil harbor scene during a pause in an international submarine rescue exercise. At bottom right a Submarine Rescue Chamber sits on the deck of a Mother Ship, with the crane used to lower/raise it behind.

These are responsible for the controlled decompression of survivors on their arrival at the surface.

The third element is the Pressurized Rescue Module System (PRMS), which is a tethered, manned Remotely Operated Rescue Vehicle (RORV) and its associated support package. These are designed to be transported by and used from vessels of opportunity (VOO). The PRMS is controlled remotely from the surface and carries two onboard attendants, who are responsible for the transfer of the survivors, and for controlling and monitoring life-support functions. The PRMS can carry up to sixteen survivors on each lift from the DISSUB to the surface.

Both the PRMS and SDS are designed for rapid deployment via air and ground transport, and for installation aboard either naval or commercial VOOs. Unlike the previous DSRV, the new system does not involve specially configured mother submarines (MOSUBs) or dedicated surface support ships, but it does include the decompression facilities lacking since the two Pigeon-class ASRs were decommissioned in 1995.

ISMERLO

A major, recent and very positive development is the establishment of the International Submarine Escape and Rescue Liaison Office (ISMERLO) on September 27, 2004, at the U.S. Navy Base at Norfolk, Virginia. During wartime, submariners on opposing sides will do their best to kill each other, but in peacetime they are always the first to offer aid, no matter what the nationality of the sunken submarine. One result of the *Kursk* tragedy in 2000 was to cause the international submarine community to examine the way it conducted its business and to realize that a great deal more coordination and information exchange was required in order to make rescues more timely and effective.

ISMERLO is a very small cell and is not intended to be an executive organization directing submarine rescues, but rather a clearing house for the exchange of information and coordination. Thus, all navies with submarine assets would know what rescue facilities were available, where they were, and how they operated. Most importantly, they would know whom to contact to obtain their services.

In addition to offering assistance it is essential that both rescuers and the rescued should understand what the other are doing, and also that equipment should meet certain common requirements. In this, NATO, as the most effective of all existing international organizations, has provided the basis for commonality, resulting in increasing adoption of the relevant Standard NATO Agreements (STANAGs), Allied Technical Publications (ATPs) and communications (Link 11). Apart from regular cooperation and working groups, there are regular international submarine rescue exercises in which participation, once restricted to NATO members, is now on a global scale.

In one typical international exercise, "Sedgemoor 2001," DSRV *Mystic* was flown by USAF C-5 Galaxy from its base at San Diego to the British airfield at Prestwick, where it was offloaded onto a wheeled transporter and taken by road to the Clyde naval base. There it was lifted by crane onto a Royal Navy SSBN, HMS *Vanguard*, and taken to the site of a simulated DISSUB, the Swedish HSwedMS *Gotland*, lying on the bottom of Raasay Sound off the Isle of Mull at a depth of some 450 feet. Having located the DISSUB, the four-man DSRV crew transferred from the *Vanguard* to *Mystic*, disengaged, and then moved the DSRV to *Gotland*, where it mated with the standard hatch. It then disengaged and returned to the *Vanguard*. Meanwhile, the British LR5 had arrived by surface MOSHIP, the Swedish HSwedMS *Belos*, and it, too, engaged with *Gotland* and accepted some Swedish submariners before disengaging, traveling a short distance and then returning them to the *Gotland* in a simulated rescue.

Left: HMS *Vanguard*, one of the United Kingdom Royal Navy's three SSBNs. Like all modern British submarines its hatches are built to full NATO standard and can be mated with any submersible fitted with the correct type of skirt.

PART VII: CONCLUSIONS

Left: This British SSN was developed during the Cold War at a time when cooperation between the major alliances was minimal. Today, however, if there is a submarine accident all navies rush to help, with cooperation made easier by the interoperability of procedures, exchange of information, and international standardization of hatches and other access points.

PART VII: CONCLUSIONS

Many submarine services have never lost a single submarine or, perhaps, not even one sailor's life, due to accidental causes, whereas a small number have suffered many losses. There are several reasons for this, the first being that, statistically, a navy with a larger number of submarines stands more chance of suffering a disaster, but this is by no means the whole story. Small navies with just a few submarines are unlikely to be pioneers trying out new designs or new technologies, but will take tried-and-tested designs in which any faults will have been found and eradicated by others. In addition, the tempo of operations in smaller navies tends to be much less intense and they undertake missions that are not only close to their bases, but also well within the limits of both submarine and crew. The largest navies, however, are always bringing new technology into service, routinely operate at a great intensity, undertake missions far from their bases, and, on occasions, deliberately take risks. They also test their potential enemies by operating close to their shores, or in close proximity to their battle groups at sea.

When accidents do occur, some navies are very public about them, either as a matter of policy or because their media are both active and investigative and leave them with little alternative than to make explanatory statements. Other navies have been deliberately secretive; thus, between 1945 and 1990 the Soviet Navy would only ever admit to submarine accidents if it was absolutely forced into doing so, and a number of hitherto completely unknown accidents were revealed only after the Cold War had ended. The Chinese Navy (PLA-N) of today follows exactly the same secretive procedures. On the other hand there have been rumors, so far unsubstantiated, that accidents occurred during that Cold War period involving Western submarines in the Barents Sea, which were hushed-up on grounds of national security.

TECHNOLOGY

Submarine technology has advanced dramatically over the past 150 years. The initial hulls were constructed of boiler-plate with some internal reinforcement, but hulls gradually became more robust, to the point where today's submarines are not only very large but are also immensely strong. It was also realized quite early that hulls not only needed to be strong, but also had to be divided into watertight compartments, so that damaged sections could be isolated, thus giving submariners a better chance of survival and escape.

There have been occasions where technological advance has brought new dangers. The snorkel, for example, enabled diesel-electric submarines to recharge their batteries while traveling below the surface, conferring a

Below: The Soviet Navy produced some adventurous designs, such as this Alfa-class, which had titanium hulls and liquid-metal reactors—and far faster than anything in the West. It also had an appalling safety record, losing many men and submarines.

Above: Launch of USS *Miami* (SSN-755) at the Electric Boat Yard at Groton, Connecticut, November 12, 1988. Since the loss of *Thresher* and *Scorpion* in the 1960s, the U.S. Navy has never lost another nuclear-powered submarine.

great tactical advantage, but a number of submarines were lost due to snorkels either malfunctioning or breaking altogether. Of even greater significance was the introduction of nuclear propulsion. This brought the inestimable advantage that submarines could remain submerged almost indefinitely, but also introduced new dangers of high-pressure steam leaks and, even worse, of nuclear irradiation for the crew and, in the worst of all scenarios, nuclear contamination of large areas of the seabed. Some other technologies have, however, proved

too hazardous; hydrogen peroxide propulsion, for example, which appeared at one time to offer an acceptable alternative to nuclear propulsion, was abandoned because it was far too difficult to handle and posed great dangers to the crew.

SURFACE COLLISIONS

Up to about the mid-1960s there were many collisions between submarines and surface ships, but it was always the submarine that came off the worst. Even when the U.S. merchant ship *Thomas Lykes* hit the French *Surcouf* submarine in 1942, the 4,000-ton submarine sank without the surface ship's crew realizing that they had hit something. One consequence of larger and more robust submarines, however, and particularly with the largest, SSNs and SSBNs, has been the reversal of fortunes, so that it is now the submarine that emerges relatively unscathed and the surface ship which is either very badly damaged or sinks. In the *Greeneville/Ehime Maru* tragedy in February 2001, for example, there was great disparity in size. In addition, the American submarine's hull was built of very high-strength steel, making it almost immeasurably

Left: The wreck of Japanese training ship *Ehime Maru* at her permanent resting-place on the seabed off Hawaii. She was rammed from below and sunk by USS *Greeneville* (SSN-722) on February 10, 2001.

SHIP	DISPLACEMENT (TONS)	LENGTH (FT)	BEAM (FT)	LAUNCHED
GREENVILLE	6,900	360	33	1996
EHIME MARU	741	180	32	1996

superior to the Japanese fisheries training ship whose hull was made of normal ship-building steel. Both were modern (launched in the same year) and well-found, but when *Greeneville*'s vertical rudder carved its way into the Japanese ship's engine room, the latter did not have a chance and sank within ten minutes, while the submarine was barely scratched.

HUMAN ERROR

Human error has been the cause of many submarine losses, sometimes through carelessness or oversight, but also due to honest mistakes, confusion or lack of training. As each example has come to light, navies have amended procedures and training programs, while designers have introduced new technical or mechanical safeguards, in order to prevent a recurrence. Thus, accidents such as leaving a hatch open or pulling the wrong lever have been steadily eliminated, but failing to follow procedures by surfacing without checking the surrounding sea for surface shipping can still occur.

TRAINING

Among the more surprising losses are those of the German *Kriegsmarine* training organization over the period 1939 to 1945. It is, of course, a well-known principle that men should "train hard, fight easy" but the U-boat arm lost a total of 25 submarines and 549 men killed during training accidents (with many more non-fatal accidents), all of which took place in the Baltic and not one of them involving the enemy.

CAUSE UNKNOWN

There were very few submarines lost to unknown causes during World War One, but World War Two saw a tremendous increase, with no fewer than 76 submarines and 4,631 men being unaccounted for. It seems a reasonable assumption that some must have been due to enemy action but, despite careful log-keeping at the time and painstaking research since, it has been impossible to reach definite conclusions. What happened to the others is quite simply a matter for speculation, running the whole gamut from navigational and other human errors to technical faults.

Occasionally a hull may be found and investigated by divers, but in the majority of such cases it is probable that nobody will ever know the cause of the disasters.

THE COLD WAR

The Cold War, which lasted from approximately 1948 to 1992, was in many ways as intense for submariners in the main navies as an open conflict. No weapons were used, but some of the hounding of the "other side's" submarines was as hostile as it would have been in a real combat. A particular factor was the extraordinary expansion of the Soviet Navy, which transformed itself over a period of some twenty to thirty years from a small, essentially coastal force into the second largest navy in the world, deployed into every ocean and at the cutting-edge of technological development. This hasty expansion happened to take place at a time of extremely rapid technological development, with the introduction of nuclear propulsion and the deployment of rocket-powered missiles. The expansion in the numbers of hulls meant that many more crewmen were required quickly, which meant that quality and standards of training and experience were diluted.

Above: The Russian Navy's Oscar-class had a good reputation until *Kursk* was literally blown apart by an explosion resulting from a leakage of hydrogen peroxide in a torpedo.

ISMERLO

Even though, as described earlier, ISMERLO (the International Submarine Escape and Rescue Liaison Office) currently has only a very small staff, the very fact of its existence marks a significant advance in international cooperation. Perhaps less obvious to the layman is the increasing standardization in matters such as the dimensions of hatches and fittings, procedures in conducting rescues, and in the exchange of information. In addition to all this, the increasing number of international exercises ensures that all aspects of rescues are rehearsed and differences or problems identified and resolved.

The value of the new arrangements was dramatically demonstrated in the August 2005 rescue of the crew of Russian mini-sub, *Priz*. This vessel was on a training exercise off the Petropavlovsk naval base on the Kamchatka peninsula, Thursday, August 4, 2005, when it became entangled with fishing-net ropes on the seabed at a depth of some 625 feet—over twice the depth at which the *Kursk* sank in 2000. In the struggle to free the craft the ropes became more tightly entangled and, at first, the Russian Navy tried to free the stricken vessel by dragging the bottom with anchors, their aim being to "catch" *Priz* and then carry it to shallower water. These attempts failed, but in the meantime both the U.S. and the UK had dispatched recovery teams and equipment. The British team, equipped with the Scorpio 7 ROV, flew from Scotland to Siberia in an RAF C-17 aircraft, landed at Petropavlovsk, and were then trucked to the nearest port, where they embarked aboard a Russian Mother Ship and were carried to the scene.

Priz is a 25-year-old submersible, intended for deep-sea operations with a crew of three, but on this occasion it had six naval men and a civilian from the shipbuilders aboard. There was only three hours air supply remaining when Scorpio 7 reached the stricken submarine. The operator aboard the rescue ship was able to maneuver the ROV using TV cameras and then cut the ropes one by one until *Priz* suddenly became free and shot to the surface. The crew, all remarkably fit and healthy after their three-day ordeal, were quickly reunited with their families.

While the British team was first on the scene and actually conducted the release operation, the credit must go to the entire international submarine community which had spent the years since the *Kursk* disaster in pooling information through ISMERLO, standardizing operating procedures, and practicing it all in regular exercises.

HUMAN TRIUMPH

In the early days, the only feasible means of rescue was collectively, by lifting the whole submarine to the surface. To be effective this required a large number of rescue ships and crews scattered around areas of possible accidents. This meant that they spent a lot of time doing nothing, and, when an accident did occur, the ships usually turned out to be in the wrong place, anyway.

The emphasis then turned to individual escape, but again this was difficult and, in many cases, the men who did escape from the stricken submarine often died either during the ascent or on the surface when the rescuers failed to find them. Gradually the problems of individual escape were resolved, but then attention turned to multiple escapes in diving bells. Thus, we have arrived at today's solutions where the aim is to achieve multiple escapes in deep-submergence rescue vessels.

Above: At the heart of every submarine is its crew and it is vital that they be given every chance of survival in the event of an accident, which can happen even in the best-regulated navies.

Above: The Russian minisub *Priz* surfaces after her dramatic rescue in 2005. The international effort involved showed the success of the modern arrangements, coordinated by ISMERLO, based at Norfolk, Virginia.

Despite all these technological advances, one element has remained totally unchanged—the human being—whose body remains as vulnerable as ever to the effects of atmospheric and hydrostatic pressure. On the other hand, it is frequently the human qualities of ingenuity, determination, courage and leadership that combine to overcome apparently insuperable obstacles. As long ago as 1851, Wilhelm Bauer showed that careful analysis of the problem, coupled with the determination and leadership to see it through, could lead to a successful rescue, and his example has been followed by many men over the following 160 years. As a result, while there have been many disasters, some of them, unfortunately, avoidable, there have also been many occasions where men have triumphed over the shortcomings of technology, the harshness of the environment in which they operate, and last, but by no means least, mistakes made by others.

Above: All modern submarines are equipped for individual escape, as with this British submariner. But collective rescue is much preferred, being more efficient and less dangerous, although there will always be a time delay in getting DSRVs or ROVs to the site.

Right: U.S. Navy *Avalon* (DSRV-2) is installed on the afterdeck of a British SSBN in preparation for a joint exercise. International exercises are conducted with great regularity around the world, giving participants and observers the opportunity to ensure that both equipment and procedures are fully compatible.

BIBLIOGRAPHY

Akermann, Paul; *Encyclopaedia of British Submarines, 1901-1955*; Maritime Press, England, 1989

Alden, J. D.; *The Fleet Submarine in the U.S. Navy*; Arms & Armour Press, London, England, 1979

Baker, A. D.; *Combat Fleets of the World*; Naval Institute Press, Annapolis, USA (various annual editions)

Blair, C.; *Hitler's U-Boat War* (2 volumes); Weidenfeld & Nicholson, London, England, 1999

Boyd, C. and Yoshida, A.; *The Japanese Submarine Force in World War II*; Airlife, Shrewsbury, England, 1996

Compton-Hall, Richard; *Submarine Boats, The Beginnings of Submarine Warfare*; Conway Maritime Press, London, England, 1983.

Conway's All The World's Fighting Ships; Volume I—1860-1905; Volume II—1906-1921; Volume III—1922-1946; Volume IV—1947-1995; Conway Maritime Press, London, England

Gabler, Ulrich; *Submarine Design*; Bernard & Graefe Verlag, Koblenz, Germany, 1986

Herzog, Bodo; *Deutsche U-boote 1906-1966*; Bernard & Graefe Verlag, Koblenz, Germany, 1990

Hessler, G.; *German Naval History—The U-Boat War in the Atlantic 1939-45*; Her Majesty's Stationery Office, London, England, 1989

Rohwer, J. and Hummelchen, G.; *Chronology of the War at Sea 1939-1945* (revised edition); Greenhill Books, London, England, 1992

Rössler, Eberhard; *The U-Boat, The Evolution and Technical History of German Submarines*; Arms & Armour Press, London, England, 1981

Wynn, K.; *U-Boat Operations of the Second World War* (2 volumes); Chatham Publishing, London, England, 1997

INDEX

PICTURE CREDITS

Abbreviations: US Naval Historical Center (NHC); Royal Navy Submarine Museum (RNSM)

Page 1: RNSM; 2-3: NHC; 4-5: RNSM; 6-7: US Navy; 8-9: NHC; 10-11: RB Collection; 12-13: RB Collection; 14-15: RNSM; 16-17: RNSM; 18-19: RB Collection; 20-21: NHC; 22-23: RB Collection; 24 (top): RNSM; 24 (bottom): NHC; 25 (inset): RNSM; 26-27: RB Collection; 28-29: RNSM; 30-31: NHC; 32-33: NHC; 34: NHC; 35 (top): NHC; 35 (bottom): RB Collection; 36: RB Collection; 37: NHC; 38-39: NHC; 40 (top): RB Collection; 40 (bottom): NHC; 41: NHC; 42 (top): RB Collection; 42 (center): RNSM; 42 (bottom): NHC; 43: RNSM; 44: NHC; 45: RNSM; 46: RB Collection; 48-49: RB Collection; 50-51: RB Collection; 52-53: RB Collection; 54: NHC; 55 (top): RB Collection; 55 (bottom): RNSM; 56: RB Collection; 57 (top): RNSM; 57 (bottom): RB Collection; 58-59: RB Collection; 62: RB Collection; 63: NHC; 64-65: RB Collection; 66: RB Collection; 67: RNSM; 68-69: RNSM; 70-71: RNSM; 72-73: RB Collection; 74-75: RB Collection; 76-77: NHC; 80: RNSM; 81: NHC; 82-83: NHC; 86-87: RB Collection; 88-89: RB Collection; 90 (top): NHC; 90 (bottom): RB Collection; 91: NHC; 92: NHC; 93: RB Collection; 94-95: RB Collection; 96-97: RB Collection; 98-99: RB Collection; 100-101: Royal Navy; 102: Getty Images; 103: RB Collection; 104 (top): Getty Images; 104 (bottom): RB Collection; 105 (top): Corbis; 105 (bottom): Getty Images; 115: RNSM; 116: RNSM; 117 (top): NHC; 117 (bottom): RNSM; 118: NHC; 119: US Navy; 120: RNSM; 122 (top): NHC; 122 (bottom): RNSM; 123: US Navy; 124: US Navy; 125: RB Collection; 126 (top): RB Collection; 126 (bottom): US Navy; 127 (top): RB Collection; 127 (bottom): Royal Swedish Navy; 128: Royal Navy; 130: US Navy; 131 (top): NHC; 131 (bottom pictures): US Navy; 132: US Navy; 133: RB Collection; 136: RB Collection; 137 (top): US Navy; 137 (bottom): Getty Images; 138: RB Collection; 139: NHC; 140: RNSM; 141: US Navy.